MW00638360

Praise for

Learning to Disagree

This wonderful, deeply personal, highly entertaining book takes readers inside the brilliant mind and loving heart of an outstanding legal scholar who wants us to grow genuine friendships, even when we have principled disagreements. Here John Inazu shares everyday encounters from law classrooms, faculty offices, local coffee shops, and life at home with his family to illustrate how challenging it is to show empathy, pursue reconciliation, and offer forgiveness in today's polarized society. Rather than demonizing people who think differently or backing away from hard conversations on divisive moral issues—the way many people do—Inazu shows us how to move into today's cultural conflicts with greater charity.

Philip Ryken, president, Wheaton College

A wonderful, quirky, beautifully written, and often quite funny ode to learning how to live with deep differences. I absolutely loved this book. John Inazu writes with the kind of verve, personality, and attention to character that made me feel like I was reading a novel. Unlike most books, this one might actually change how you argue, fight, love, and even hope. It's that good.

Shadi Hamid, columnist and editorial board member, *Washington Post*; author, *The Problem of Democracy*

Not only helpful, but an absolute delight to read. In a time when there are so few examples of nuance and compassion, John Inazu's voice is one to pay close attention to.

Justin Whitmel Earley, business lawyer; speaker; bestselling author, *Made for People* and *Habits of the Household*

Using his law school classroom and personal anecdotes, John Inazu highlights the values of empathy, compassion, forgiveness, and looking for the good in others as some of the most important tools for navigating disagreements in ways that do not dehumanize those whose viewpoints may be different from one's own. As a college president whose role is to cultivate a campus environment that welcomes and supports a multitude of perspectives, I find *Learning to Disagree* to be a valuable resource for institutional leaders, as well as for professors who wish to enhance their classroom learning environment and those who facilitate professional development workshops related to dialogues across differences.

Lori S. White, PhD, president, DePauw University

Learning to Disagree

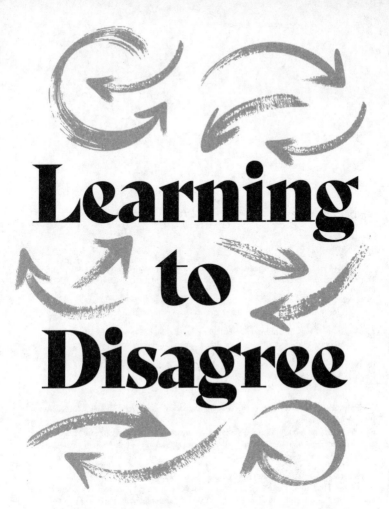

Learning to Disagree

THE SURPRISING PATH TO NAVIGATING
DIFFERENCES WITH EMPATHY AND RESPECT

John Inazu

ILLUSTRATIONS BY JOHN HENDRIX

ZONDERVAN
BOOKS

ZONDERVAN BOOKS

Learning to Disagree
Copyright © 2024 by John Inazu

Published in Grand Rapids, Michigan, by Zondervan. Zondervan is a registered trademark of The Zondervan Corporation, L.L.C., a wholly owned subsidiary of HarperCollins Christian Publishing, Inc.

Requests for information should be addressed to customercare@harpercollins.com.

Zondervan titles may be purchased in bulk for educational, business, fundraising, or sales promotional use. For information, please email SpecialMarkets@Zondervan.com.

ISBN 978-0-310-36801-4 (hardcover)
ISBN 978-0-310-36803-8 (audio)
ISBN 978-0-310-36802-1 (ebook)

All Scripture quotations, unless otherwise indicated, are taken from The Holy Bible, New International Version®, NIV®. Copyright © 1973, 1978, 1984, 2011 by Biblica, Inc.® Used by permission of Zondervan. All rights reserved worldwide. www.Zondervan.com. The "NIV" and "New International Version" are trademarks registered in the United States Patent and Trademark Office by Biblica, Inc.®

Published in association with the literary agency of Legacy LLC.

Cover design: Faceout Studio, Jeff Miller
Cover illustrations: Yulia Ogneva / Shutterstock
Interior illustrations: John Hendrix
Interior design: Denise Froehlich

Printed in the United States of America

24 25 26 27 28 LBC 5 4 3 2 1

To Caroline

Contents

Foreword

It is now almost a cliché to speak of America's increasing polarization. Multiple studies have shown that Americans have a growing disdain for those who differ from them politically and ideologically. A 2020 Brown University study found that the US is polarizing faster and more intensely than other democratic nations. More and more, we deride our political, religious, and ideological opponents as dangerous or evil and retreat to digital foxholes, lobbing insults at the "other side" to the applause of those who already agree with us.

In my work as a weekly Opinion writer at the *New York Times*, it became clear that a significant number of people truly do divide the world neatly into good and bad, liberators and oppressors. They do not want people with beliefs they find abhorrent to exist in the public square. They feel the only way forward as a nation is to stamp out those with whom they disagree. Compromise and understanding then are often seen as weakness or lack of commitment to a cause or belief. But this is folly and taken to its conclusion will inevitably lead to violence. We need a better way to live together amid irreconcilable views of God, truth, morality, and justice.

There are also people—I believe, many of us—who feel sorrow and worry over increased civic animosity, polarization, and heated rhetoric. We want a better way. Americans are increasingly lonely. We don't know our neighbors. Many of us are concerned about the future of our society. We want—and desperately need—help figuring out how to move forward and repair our fraying social fabric. We need guides to help us learn to nurture relationships and coalitions across differences, to practice civic grace.

My friend John Inazu is such a guide. In this volume, he offers a way of being in the world—a way that takes convictions seriously and takes our differences seriously, but also makes space for humility, friendship, good humor, and curiosity.

Amid the deep divisions in our world, what's clear is that it is not enough to merely extol the virtues of pluralism and loving our neighbors. We can't merely think our way to a better, healthier society—a society in which we know how to disagree well. Embracing convictions with both confidence and humility is a skill and a habit, a way of being that is practiced and grows over time. Learning to be a good neighbor, friend, and coworker across deep differences is often more like learning to walk than it is learning a creed. It is an embodied art of relating to others and to the world around us. It requires us to embrace empathy in practical ways, to allow others to have the last word, to show kindness to those who may not even like us, to seek and find our common humanity in the warp and woof of daily life. It is a practice, a craft, a dance, a vibe, a mode of living. We therefore must learn to practice civic virtues in our own context and everyday lives.

Because of this, John doesn't just tell us that a convicted and kind pluralism is vital to the health of society; he brings us into the ordinary and mundane rhythms of his life as a legal scholar, a public thinker, a professor, a dad, a friend, a coworker, a church member, and a neighbor. In the granularity of these relationships and conversations, he shows how healthy disagreement is not only possible but is, in fact, the very path to wisdom, virtue, and love.

If my friend John has one gift, it is the gift of "complexifying" things we tend to make overly simple. As his buddy, this drives me crazy at times. I will call John, full of self-righteous indignation and overconfident in my own views of an issue or idea, and he immediately asks hard questions that make me think. He cites two law cases and three personal stories that make me less sure I'm right. He deflates my ego like a sad balloon—this is a good thing if one is after wisdom, truth, and grace, though not so fun if you are after that piquant feeling of smug, superficial sanctimony.

In *Learning to Disagree*, John's gift is on display. His expertise; longtime work on pluralism; profound understanding of law, policy, and justice; and the complexity of his own family history make him well-equipped to challenge us in ways we need to be challenged. John calls us to think more deeply, to ask better questions of ourselves and others, to shed worn presumptions. He wades into the complexity of divergent ideologies he encounters every day in his classroom and work and graciously invites us to have a front-row seat. In doing so, he challenges each of us to think more deeply about what we believe and about the limits of each of our knowledge and perspective. He offers us a thoroughly accessible guide to a better civic life. These pages are a field guide to the joyful, hopeful, and necessary task of learning to disagree in a way that, in the end, teaches us to flourish.

Tish Harrison Warren,
author of *Liturgy of the Ordinary*
and *Prayer in the Night*

Preface

The book you are about to read takes you through a year of my life as a law professor. But this isn't just a book about law or legal education. It's about finding nuance and empathy in some of our country's most divisive issues. It's about holding together clarity and ambiguity, tolerance and judgment, confidence and uncertainty. It's about what each of us confronts in our daily encounters with beliefs and viewpoints we find unfamiliar, off-putting, or even dangerous.

This book won't tell you what to believe, but it does aim to change the way you engage with disagreement. The stories and vignettes are meant to complicate your assumptions, introduce arguments from "the other side," and illustrate how people can recognize good faith disagreements without surrendering their most strongly held beliefs. Millions of Americans think that politics and people are more complicated than the talking points of partisans. *Learning to Disagree* gives voice to the tone and substance of the kinds of conversations most people actually want to have.

Each chapter asks a question that emerges through a mosaic of experiences inside and outside the classroom—the cases and concepts I teach my students, my interactions with colleagues, and various life encounters outside of my day job. The classroom stories draw from my twelve years of researching and teaching Criminal Law, Law and Religion, and the First Amendment. The extracurricular stories occurred over these same years but draw from my everyday interactions with colleagues, neighbors, and friends. In this sense, this book explores not only the challenges of legal education but also the challenges all of us face in our daily lives—the complexity of people, the importance of compassion, and the pitfalls and possibilities of living in a diverse society.

The stories are true, though in reality they unfolded across several different years. Most of the characters are composites; the coffee shops are real. The stories raise difficult issues, like how we punish people who have committed unspeakable crimes, how we navigate religious diversity, and whether forgiveness is possible. They also raise fundamentally human inquiries, like searching for empathy, struggling to discern what's fair, and asking what happens when compromise isn't possible.

You can use the reflection guide at the end of this book to explore how these inquiries apply to your own life. You might work through the guide with a friend or a group of friends. The questions are meant to spark conversations more than point you toward answers. I hope you will read slowly and linger on the stories that challenge you and the claims that irritate you.

More importantly, I hope this book provides ideas and tools to navigate the differences and disagreements you encounter in our world. That's part of the goal of legal education. And while law school isn't for everyone, you may find that the lessons in this book have a surprising relevance to your own life.

How Do We Learn Empathy?

Empathy is seeing with the eyes
of another, listening with the
ears of another, and feeling
with the heart of another.

Alfred Adler

August

is absurdly humid, but the mornings offer some momentary respite, especially with a light breeze like the one I feel today. I am sitting in my favorite chair on my screened porch, a coffee mug in one hand and my cell phone in the other. If I bothered to look up from my phone, I would probably notice leafy trees and bright goldfinches. Instead, my attention on this Monday morning is fixated on the glowing screen in front of me. A lengthy social media thread about abortion is unfolding between two of my colleagues who have very different views of the world. Both of them teach constitutional law, and they both know something about the underlying legal issues in the Supreme Court's abortion cases. Social media sufficiently masks their expertise.

I really should be at my office putting the final touches on my first class of the semester. Tomorrow I'll meet eighty first-year students for their introduction to law school, and my last few pages of notes aren't going to write themselves. Plus, the short walk from my house to campus usually puts me in a good mood as I stroll past Gothic architecture and really nice grass. But the heated abortion thread keeps me planted in my chair.

I tell myself I'm scrolling through social media to catch up on the latest news. After all, my job requires some basic awareness of what's going on in the world, and the Supreme Court has certainly made its share of news in recent months. On the other hand, if social media were really about professional development, I would be much better at skipping past the sensational and snarky exchanges. You've probably been there too. You hop online to check a sports score or read your favorite columnist, and twenty minutes later you're swimming in a sea of celebrity gossip, useless factoids, and political outrage.

In addition to its unending distractions, social media also makes it harder to empathize with others. Depersonalized wars of words mediated through these two-dimensional screens obscure the complexity of other human beings. Worse still, the bots and other artificial accounts now flooding the zone mean that some of our interactions are not even with other people. If we don't pay attention, we will find that algorithms reflecting our worst impulses condition us toward animosity rather than empathy.

Some of my colleagues are less worried. They share quite a few of their opinions and feelings online—tirades against Supreme Court justices, exuberant celebrations when their team scores a political victory, despondent laments when the other team wins. I understand the impulse. I feel it too. But our students are watching. And we're training lawyers, not activists.

Legal education is not flashy. It involves exhaustive research, precise writing, and attention to language—not witty one-liners and clever retorts. This detail-oriented work is not for everyone. And—spoiler alert—legal practice is more of the same. I'm impressed that the geniuses in Hollywood keep pumping out movies about lawyers solving exotic mysteries or tracking down evil villains. Most lawyering is more mundane. Yes, some people get to channel their inner thespian every so often in the courtroom. But even trial lawyers spend most of their time in an office writing briefs, filing motions, and reviewing documents. My ten-year-old son, Sam, often reminds me of the nature of legal work: "All you do is read and write, read and write, read and write. It's so incredibly boring."

Teaching law means teaching clarity and precision, and parts of that *are* boring. But teaching law also means teaching empathy. And that's why I find the professor social media rants so jarring. They model empathy for allies and hatred for adversaries. Good lawyering requires empathy for adversaries. You don't have to *like* the other side, but you do have to understand them. How can you anticipate your opponent's reactions and next moves? And how are you going to persuade a judge or other decision maker that you have the better story?

This kind of empathy is not just for the courtroom. You can also apply it to everyday disagreements with the people you encounter in your life. Find out what motivates them. Examine how their arguments get off the ground. Ask why the conclusions that seem so obviously correct to you seem so obviously wrong to them.

Law school complicates these questions by pushing for empathy in the midst of uncertainty. These three years of education will introduce ambiguity into everything from ordinary words to deeply held beliefs. Life is suddenly full of uncertainty. Is that a legal contract? It depends. Is it murder? It depends. Is today Tuesday? It depends.

This ambiguity is especially hard for students who studied math or science in college. I majored in civil engineering, where "It depends" is rarely the right answer. The bridge either bears the load or it doesn't; the flood zone handles the water surge or it doesn't. There are plenty of unknowns and risks in engineering. But the answers to these uncertainties are usually found in mathematical equations. The law's answers to uncertainties are based on human judgment, which is why law is more art than science and why some legal decisions are politicized or biased. Some, but not all. It depends.

This uneasy world of gray is difficult to grasp after a bunch of classes in multivariable calculus and organic chemistry. The English majors who lost sleep over the meaning of Dickinson poems are much better positioned for the vagaries of law school. But college majors don't really matter that much. In a few weeks, most of these students will be equally disillusioned and dejected.

Okay, maybe not *dejected*. It's not like we're putting them through military basic training. Most of us are not yelling at them. Most of the pressures are self-imposed. And there is very little physical exertion, unless you count keeping your eyes open through endless amounts of reading.

The first year of law school does, however, resemble basic training in its indoctrination. Our slightly immodest goal is to get you to think differently and to see the world differently.

My contribution is teaching Criminal Law. It's a required course at most schools, and it's often the only first-year course that teaches statutory interpretation—how to read, understand, and argue about laws on the books. It's also a course with a lot of disturbing content. Most of the people who make their way onto the pages of Criminal Law textbooks have done awful things to other people. And my students and I will spend a semester walking through their actions and the consequences of those actions.

I glance up at a chirping goldfinch just outside my porch and realize I have now been pondering the dynamics of law school for quite some time. At least I have put down my phone to notice the goldfinch. But it is about time to head into the office.

Today is the first day of classes. I have spent the past few hours in my office reviewing the opening cases. I head down to a large room with stadium seating filled with nervous bodies and faces. A few minutes before the start of class, I walk up to the podium to set up my notes. Occasionally I look out at the anxious chatter in front of me and am greeted by quick glances and half smiles.

Once we get under way, I share a few welcome announcements and attempt a few jokes. The half-hearted nervous laughter assures me the jokes are not funny enough to ease the tension. I then turn to the dreaded "cold call." This time-honored tradition means that rather than asking for volunteers, I pepper an unlucky student with a series of pointed questions. I am part of a kinder, gentler generation of law faculty who don't find the cold call as magical as some of our predecessors did—I'm not Professor Kingsfield in *The Paper Chase* or Annalise Keating in *How to Get Away with Murder*. Still, a few light cold calls here and there are useful to hold attention spans. Besides, all of my colleagues do at least a bit of cold calling in their first-year classes. Indoctrination works best with reinforcement.

I tell my students not to lose sleep over cold calls.

Yes, they're awkward and nerve-wracking. And yes, you'll probably always remember your first one. But by the end of the semester, nobody else is going to remember what you said. Most of your classmates are too busy worrying about whether they understand the case, trying to figure out why I asked a particular question, or pretending to take notes while squeezing in some online shopping.

My first cold call falls on Stephanie Jenkins, a short blonde woman with a slight Southern accent. She's sitting six rows back in the middle of the room. Stephanie hides her nerves well, leaning back a bit in her seat and twirling a pencil with her fingers. I've learned from my preclass survey that she graduated from Davidson with a political science degree and spent two years with Teach for America.

"Stephanie, tell us the facts of *Dudley and Stephens*."

Dudley and Stephens is nearly a rite of passage in law school. It involves a nineteenth-century murder prosecution in England: four guys on a boat get lost at sea and run out of food and water with no rescue in sight; they are all very hungry; three of them kill and eat the fourth, a poor soul named Parker.

My opening question to Stephanie is a total softball. After all, how could you forget *those* facts? Some cases are hard to keep straight, but most of these students will remember *Dudley and Stephens* for the rest of their lives. Stephanie remembers the facts and stumbles admirably through her first law school cold call.

After Stephanie sets the stage, we dig a little deeper. Are all three men equally culpable? Or is the guy who hatched the plan better or worse than the guy who took the knife to

Parker? And what about the third guy who just watched it all go down but admittedly partook of the body? Think about it for a minute. Put yourself in that boat and pay attention to who is doing what around you. How should the law assign responsibility to the people who have committed these awful deeds?

Then we take it to another level. What if these actions aren't even blameworthy? "Stephanie, is there any way to *justify* the actions of these three men?"

At this point in the semester, it's important to finesse my question. So after a slight pause, I add, "In other words, is there an argument that these men did the right thing by eating Parker? Or at least that their actions were tolerable?"

"Well," Stephanie offers tentatively, "perhaps we could argue for the greater good—that it's better to sacrifice one life to save three."

"Maybe," I respond, "but how do we determine the greater good? What if Parker were a Nobel Prize researcher on the brink of curing a major disease and the other three were violent terrorists?"

"And," she adds, already second-guessing her initial answer, "it's probably never a good idea to describe killing an innocent person as a morally good action."

A few others chime in, and it soon becomes apparent to the class that there is no easy formula to tell us that killing and eating Parker was the right thing to do.

Dudley and Stephens is a wild case, and I have to remind myself that not everyone in the room has read it as often as I have. The first time through can be a bit jarring. That's one reason some Criminal Law professors have cut it from the curriculum. The other reason is that these days, there just aren't many cases of cannibalism on the high seas. Wouldn't our time be better spent on something more commonplace, like drug possession crimes? Maybe so, and in any event, we'll get to some of those later in the course. But I'm not giving up on *Dudley and Stephens*. I like the case because it takes us to the limits of empathy.

At first glance, these limits come from intuition. Killing and eating people is bad; good people don't do those things; we would never do those things. But I want my students to wrestle with a more unsettling question: *How do you know?* I get grumpy when I skip lunch. Some of my students have experienced greater hunger, but most of them haven't missed more than a few meals in a row. And I'm fairly certain that none of us have been stranded in the ocean for days without food and water.

This brings me to another question for Stephanie. "Even if these three men are morally and legally blameworthy, could we conclude that they should nevertheless escape punishment?"

Stephanie pauses for a moment, twirling her pencil and curling her lip before speaking.

"Maybe they've already been punished enough."

It's a smart insight. Maybe this particular situation is so extraordinary, so impossible to comprehend, that we really have no idea how normal people—people like us—would respond. These poor guys have been through hell and back. They lost their ship, nearly starved to death, and then killed and ate a guy in a very small boat.

The truth is that we have no idea what we would have done in their shoes. Stephanie's answer suggests why the limits of our own experiences might cause us to question—or at least slow down—some of our judgments. Rather than launching into an immediate critique of how someone else has handled an unfamiliar or impossible situation, we might pause to imagine the distance that divides our experiences. We may find after a little reflection that we aren't as sure as we initially thought. Sometimes a drop of empathy can restrain a flood of needless words and thoughtless commentary.

Law school provides plenty of opportunities to practice this restraint through a series of clashing perspectives that emerge from different experiences. What happens when a white student from rural Missouri and a black student from Chicago find themselves debating police shootings? How do students of different faiths and no faith navigate difficult questions about the limits of religious practice? How do students discuss the legal contours of abortion, immigration, and affirmative action with peers across the political spectrum? Law school teaches a set of professional skills, but it also teaches students how to relate to one another—how to find empathy across differences.

You don't have to be wired like a lawyer to learn these skills. Empathy is not rocket science. It's hearing an unfamiliar or off-putting argument, pausing to think about what's been said, and responding with an appropriately engaged question. It's giving people the benefit of the doubt because you may not know what battles they are fighting. It's treating others the way you would like to be treated. Empathy is the simple stuff that's hard to put into practice.

Law school highlights another reason for empathy—the better you understand the other side of an argument, the better you can critique it and the more strongly you can defend your own position. If all you do is reflexively dismiss the other side ("Those idiots—how could anyone think that way? What a stupid idea!"), you will never really understand the argument someone is making or why they are making it. Attributing bad arguments to people you think are dumb is easy, but it usually misleads you. Empathy lets you see that smart and well-intentioned people can also make bad arguments.

The next afternoon, I am giving a welcome talk to the first-year class. The dean has asked me to speak about free speech norms. The school has crammed all three hundred first-year students into a lecture hall with seats that look like they're built for middle schoolers. Despite our tight quarters, the students seem more relaxed for today's talk, probably because they know there won't be any cold calls and none of this material is showing up on an exam. Still, I am glad we have these talks in the first few weeks of the semester. It's good to lay a common foundation.

After a relatively quiet start to my presentation, I get a few laughs with a slide about halfway through that reads, "Don't be a First Amendment hero." The point is simple enough. Yes, you are legally permitted to say almost anything to almost anyone. The First Amendment protects your right to say all kinds of terrible, life-destroying words. But just because you can say whatever you want doesn't mean you should. Making the most offensive or outlandish comment to prove a point or test a principle is seldom going to win you supporters, to say nothing of friends. And lawyers—including lawyers-in-training—should know the importance of persuasion.

Unfortunately, law school has no shortage of First Amendment heroes. Sometimes they're conservative agitators trying to "own the libs" by pushing speech norms to the brink of acceptability—mocking gay people, feminists, or whatever other group they think is most privileged in higher education. But conservatives don't have a monopoly on incivility. I have heard plenty of liberal rants around the law school that fail the test of basic decency—tirades against police officers, conservative religious believers, and Republican voters, among others. In these cases, it's as though liberal tolerance reaches its limit when it comes to nonliberal views.

My challenge to these first-year students to speak charitably is complicated by their diverse backgrounds. They come from different communities and ways of life. Some of them have rarely interacted with people of different races, religions, or political backgrounds. Some of them laughed comfortably a few months ago at jokes they wouldn't dare share publicly now; others are more emboldened to say things they carefully suppressed back home. Over the next three years, these students will confront the limits of their own experiences through interactions with peers in and out of the classroom. Sometimes these limits will come to light through harsh words or emotional reactions. At other times the signals will be subtler—the raised eyebrow, the tensed shoulders, the glistening eye. Some of these students will worry about being ostracized by their peers; others will muster the courage to challenge unquestioned assumptions. They will all wrestle with striking an appropriate balance between lamentable self-censorship and laudable compassion.

I suggest to the students in front of me that the right approach lies at the intersection of civic responsibility and civic grace: don't be afraid to express your honest opinions but treat others kindly. I want these students to care about their words and take seriously the responsibility that comes with free speech. But I also want them to question orthodoxies and engage when others are too intimidated to do so. Some corners of law school cultivate the First Amendment heroes we don't need; others suppress speech because they can't imagine reasonable disagreement with their own viewpoints.

Many of us encounter these same competing pressures in our daily lives. In some contexts, we are too flippant with our words, not realizing how our choice of language or attempts at humor affect others in the room. Elsewhere, we are too conscious of what we say, too worried that forgetting the currently fashionable language norms will lead to critical glares and hushed condemnations.

I illustrate these ideas in my talk with the debate over gender pronouns. These days, some people want to be called by their preferred pronouns, a reflection of rapidly changing understandings of gender in our society. Other people feel that doing so will force them to speak untruthfully about the world. Recognizing the underlying tension is a good first step toward discerning what to do in these circumstances. Sometimes language itself gives us a way out of challenges that come from language. When it comes to the pronoun showdown, proper names can often go a long way toward sidestepping controversy. Instead of worrying about my pronouns, you can just call me "John"—or if you are my student, the gender-neutral "Professor" works fine. You don't always have to engage in the culture fight. And every time you choose to interact with someone in a way that neither downplays your own beliefs nor raises their hackles, you have made a small step toward building a kinder and gentler world around you.

After my First Amendment presentation, a couple of students walk to the front of the room to introduce themselves. I guess correctly from their mannerisms that they are both military veterans. Staff Sergeant (retired) Patricia Smith and Ensign Joseph Villario discovered their common connection at last week's orientation. Smith is a former Army helicopter mechanic, medically retired after a training accident crushed her arm. She's trying law as a second career. Villario is here on a Navy-funded program before returning to active duty as a military lawyer.

I'm drawn to the veterans in part because I am one, which is rare among law professors. I went to college on an ROTC scholarship and spent four years as an Air Force lawyer at the Pentagon. My son Sam regularly reminds me that this isn't actually cool. "It's not like you flew jets, Dad. You just worked a desk."

Less than one percent of law professors are veterans, and that rate probably holds across other academic disciplines. It's a noticeable shift from faculty demographics a few generations ago. Even as higher education has rightly diversified across a number of categories, we've become less diverse when it comes to veterans. It's true of Congress as well, and the veteran gap skews socioeconomically too. You may have sensed this watching the news or seeing who shows up for military funerals in your own community.

Smith and Villario share a few stories and make their obligatory jabs about the Air Force being the cushier service. Then they invite me to join them on a morning run with the student veterans club. A good rule of thumb is never to run with people half your age, unless you're a really good runner. I politely decline the invitation, fumbling through some excuse about having to prepare for classes. "No problem, sir. We'll be sure to reach out on some other occasion." The veterans are the only people who call me "sir" anymore. And if "some other occasion" means "not running," then I'm in.

Talking with Smith and Villario reminds me of the unique perspective veterans bring to law school. Smith spent nine months in the Middle East and had her base hit a couple of times by insurgents. Villario lost a couple of guys working for him when a fire broke out on his ship. These kinds of experiences put into perspective some of the pressures of reading cases and writing briefs.

On the way back to my office, I bump into my colleague Brenda Williams—a tall black woman in her late thirties. Brenda's main research area is tax policy and housing inequality. She has been on the faculty for fifteen years after completing law school at Yale, a fancy appellate clerkship, and a few years at the Department of Justice. Law professors are generally high on ego and low on social skills. Brenda has her share of ego but hides it well with above average social skills. We are friends, but we don't spend much time together outside of work.

Brenda, as it turns out, is on her way to give her own orientation talk to the first-year students; hers is on understanding bias. The basic gist of her message is that our experiences and assumptions create bias, and many of us are prone to act on that bias in unhelpful ways. Sometimes bias manifests as overt prejudice. I have seen enough outright bias to know that it knows no ideological bounds. It is most acute when I find myself *passing* as part of the in-group—the white people at the fancy restaurant who don't pick up that I am half-Japanese, the secular colleagues who can't imagine I actually believe in God, the conservative religious neighbors who assume I share their politics. I am amazed at the things people say when they think everyone listening is just like them.

Maybe you've experienced this too. Maybe you have a hidden or less visible identity regarding your faith, politics, or sexuality, and you've found yourself in rooms where nobody seems to realize you might be different. It's worth remembering how you felt about the careless words and thoughtless jokes you heard.

If we're honest with ourselves, most of us could work toward greater consistency between what we say publicly and what we say privately. That doesn't mean we have to censor ourselves all the time or hold back our true beliefs in trusted circles—that would be an exhausting way to live. But it might mean that we pay more attention to our words and our jokes even in the more informal parts of our lives, realizing that doing so could help us lead more authentic and integrated lives. In fact, if we use greater care and compassion in our informal conversations, we may find ourselves worrying less about "saying the wrong thing" in more public settings.

These issues of bias are extremely important, but I am not convinced that bias training is the right way to address them. Judging from some of the recent research, I'm not alone. In addition to questions about its efficacy, much of this training feels rote and performative. I've been in meetings where everyone in the room has clearly been through dozens of these, and some of my colleagues still offer public laments at the end of our time:

> **Jill from Political Science:** *"I realized anew, much to my horror, that I still have bias."*
> **Ben from English:** *"I thought I had overcome my biases, but this important training makes me realize how far I still have to go."*
> **Laurie, no idea what department she's in or why she's at this meeting:** *"I hope we can all do better with our bias in the future."*

Brenda's talk to the law students differs from the standard bias training and draws more from her own life experiences. Her stories are powerful, and she is also a captivating speaker. But even the best talk only scratches the surface. Working on bias is going to take pushing through abstract categories to get to actual people whose contradictions and imperfections defy stereotypes and labels.

Like the stereotypes and labels I am now realizing I projected onto Smith and Villario a few minutes ago. In sizing up the two of them, I assumed that veterans will not feel the pressure of law school as intensely as others around them. But while some veterans arrive at law school strong and resilient, others are traumatized and disoriented. Some veterans navigate academic pressures with ease; others struggle and even despair. Empathy, I am reminded, attaches to people, not abstractions.

I have modest confidence that my students will learn something about empathy during their time in law school. They will have the luxury of exploring nuance and difference with each other for the next three years. It's not life in the foxhole, but it's closer quarters with a diverse group than many of them will experience in other parts of their lives.

Legal education at its best teaches the tools of disagreement and provides plenty of opportunities to put those tools into practice. But you don't have to be in law school to learn these skills. You can begin to recognize the complexity of the people around you and the empathy this complexity can bring to you. You can start by assuming the best of someone—or at least not assuming the worst—to open the door to deeper understanding and an opportunity to learn from those who see the world differently.

Can We Know
What's Fair?

People don't always get what
they deserve in this world.

Lemony Snicket

The first few weeks of the semester disappear in a frenzy of learning students' names and hunting down classroom amenities such as microphones and erasers. There's also a lingering fear as I begin to write on the board each morning that what I think is a dry erase marker is a permanent one. I've never actually made this mistake, but the accidental graffiti that adorns every whiteboard in the law school is a constant reminder that it can happen to anyone.

The other challenge this time of year is helping a few overeager students find their place in our classroom ecosystem. In law school, we call them gunners. Every class has a couple of gunners—the students who are a little too ready to participate, a little too self-absorbed. The gunners usually sit toward the front of the class, and they raise their hands incessantly. Some of them are brilliantly focused, and others are hopelessly lost. Most of them lack the ability to read a room.

Law school fixates on individual performance, but few gunners will make great lawyers. Great lawyers need to play well in the sandbox, and that means, among other things, something closer to a Goldilocks approach to speaking in class. There is no set formula, but part of it is based on class size: talk more in smaller classes; talk less in larger ones. Yes, you may be paying a lot of money and spending a lot of time to be here, but so is everyone else. This class doesn't exist for you; it exists for a larger group of which you are a part. Think of it as an exercise in fairness.

Of course, what counts as fair is not always obvious. And this is true in situations with a lot more on the line than who speaks in class. What's the fair tax policy in our country? What's the fair level of immigration or the fair amount of disaster relief? What's the fair punishment for killing someone? We take up this last question in Thursday's Criminal Law class.

I lay the groundwork with some basic terminology. "Manuel, can you tell me the difference between a homicide and a criminal killing?"

Manuel, a stocky, deep-voiced kid from the Bronx, has done the readings and knows this first question is just a warm-up: "A homicide is when a person kills another person. But not all homicides are crimes," he says assuredly.

"Right." Even in this initial exchange, Manuel and I have already made an important distinction too often lost in sensationalist media coverage of tragic deaths. Once you know the difference, you'll start to see it everywhere. "The coroner announced that the woman's death was a homicide" tells us nothing about whether a crime occurred—it just means that the woman was killed by another human being.

"Manuel, what are some examples of homicides that aren't crimes?"

"Killing in justified self-defense, killing an enemy combatant in a lawful war, a police officer who kills acting under color of law."

At this point, Manuel is reading directly from the text,

which I know because he is using words like *justified*, *lawful*, and *acting under color of law* just a few weeks into law school. But this verbatim language is exactly what I'm looking for in this part of the discussion. I take the opportunity to highlight the importance of these qualifying words. For example, when a police officer fatally shoots a suspect, we need a lot more information before we can determine whether the shooting is unjustified and unlawful—before we can know whether the homicide is a crime. That is one reason it's seldom productive to jump to conclusions based on breaking news. You should usually wait a bit to collect more facts.

My colloquy with Manuel also introduces an important distinction between facts and judgments. A homicide is a fact of the world. Whether that homicide is a crime is a judgment. That judgment depends on what the law says, what the evidence shows, and how the people charged with applying those laws to that evidence make their decisions. And those people—police officers, prosecutors, judges, and juries—aren't always going to get it right.

Manuel and I turn to the next level of complexity. "Manuel, what are some examples of criminal homicides that aren't murders?"

"Accidental killings?"

"Right. Some people kill unintentionally. They're careless or reckless, but they don't intend to kill anyone. The death they caused might still be a crime, but it's not murder. Sometimes it's closer to manslaughter."

The law cares about these distinctions, and it reflects them in the ways it punishes criminal homicides. Murder is usually worse than manslaughter. If I kill you purposely, I'm usually more blameworthy than if I kill you recklessly. Usually, but not always. And this is where things get really interesting.

I ask the class to think of a man—let's call him Steve—who induces his friend to play a variant of Russian roulette known as Russian poker. Participants in this morbid game take turns pointing a loaded gun at each other and pulling the trigger. There's only one bullet in the chamber, which means that each turn of the game brings a one in six chance of someone dying.

Suppose Steve pulls the trigger, the bullet fires, and his friend dies. Steve did not intend to kill his friend—in fact, the overwhelming odds were that his friend was not going to die. By all accounts, the death was an accident. But some states will punish Steve more severely than they would punish a "regular" reckless accidental killer like a drunk driver. In other words, they will treat Steve like a murderer rather than an accidental killer.

This state of the world raises a fascinating set of questions. Reckless homicides are already pretty bad. The statutes describe them as showing "wanton disregard for human life." But they usually do not get punished like murder. So how is it fair to punish Steve, a reckless killer, at the same level that we punish an intentional killer? Is it because most of us are repulsed by the idea of Russian poker? Would we feel the same if Steve successfully persuaded his friend to attempt to summit Nanga Parbat in the Himalayas, which brings roughly the same odds of death as Russian poker?

I ask Manuel about the example of celebratory gunfire. Think of the guy who shoots a gun into the air after a big sports win or on the Fourth of July. Suppose the bullet kills a bystander on the way down. Do we punish that guy like Steve, the Russian poker player, or do we think the guy shooting his gun in the air is closer to a "regular" reckless killer?

Manuel pauses for a moment and then responds, "I think that's closer to murder. There's no reason for someone to die because some guy is celebrating."

"But he had no intent to kill. He was just shooting a gun into the air. Is that really as bad as murder?"

Jenna, a tall, slender woman from Cooke County, Tennessee, sitting off to the right of the classroom, jumps into the discussion. "When I was growing up, we fired guns into the air all the time, and nobody thought twice about it. There's no way that guy is a murderer." I detect a slight note of irritation in Jenna's voice.

Jim—at least I think his name is Jim—raises his hand from the back row. "Who gets to decide what counts as fair?" He continues, "What if a recent immigrant fires a gun into the air because that's how they always celebrated in his home country? Does the law hold him to a standard he has no way of knowing exists?"

I love this question from maybe Jim. It highlights the cultural assumptions embedded in a bedrock legal concept like fairness. What's fair and reasonable, it turns out, has a lot to do with our own experiences and sense of the world.

I tell Jim that these questions of fairness get even harder. Most people speed, which is to say that most people engage in reckless and illegal behavior. Some of us have sped really fast or texted while driving—actions that might be not only reckless but *really* reckless. But even if we accidentally kill someone while driving recklessly, we don't think of ourselves like we think of Steve, the Russian poker guy. We punish Steve differently to send a message—reckless behavior that kills people is bad, but *some* reckless behavior that kills people is *really* bad.

But what if Steve does not fully comprehend his actions? What if he is ten years old with no knowledge of how to use a gun, or ninety years old with dementia? It turns out that in circumstances like these, the law *excuses* really reckless behavior instead of punishing it.

So let's get this straight. Murder is usually worse than killing someone on accident. But some accidental killings are so reckless we punish them like murders. Unless the reckless killers are so abnormal that we don't hold them accountable for their actions—then we don't punish them at all.

Does any of this sound fair to you? Let's make it even harder, with another example I share with my class. In 2011, Jennifer Axelberg was arrested for driving drunk in rural Minnesota. She and her husband had been drinking with friends at a remote lake cabin when he began beating her on the head. At two in the morning, she ran to her car, and he chased after her. Once she was in the car, he pounded on the windshield so hard it began to shatter. She had no cell phone—he had taken it from her. So she drove away to find safety.

Do you think of Jennifer's drunk driving in the same way you think of a college student who drives after drinking too much at a party? What if Jennifer had struck and killed someone while fleeing her husband? What if she had driven through a crowded sidewalk but managed not to hurt anyone? When we ask these kinds of questions, we begin to realize that our intuitions about fairness reflect not only Jennifer's actions but also her motives, the risk she created, and the actual harm she caused. All of these factors suggest that the context surrounding our actions affects how we assess their blameworthiness.

These tensions and ambiguities also highlight the uncomfortable reality that while the law is a useful and necessary social tool, it does not and cannot answer all of our questions about fairness. Try putting yourself—or your daughter, sister, or friend—in Jennifer Axelberg's shoes. What would you do, and how would you want the law to treat you?

Laws and courts will reach decisions about some of these cases. They will tell us what is going to happen. But they won't always tell us what *should* happen. Sometimes questions of what should happen—questions of fairness—lack clear answers. The law is not going to tell us what should happen to Steve, the Russian poker player. It won't tell us what should happen to Jennifer, the drunk driver. And it's not going to tell us what should happen to the drunk Marine.

I learn about the drunk Marine from Charlie Singleton, a broad-shouldered blond guy with a short beard and a gregarious smile. He approaches me the day after I bring up Jennifer Axelberg and asks that I not call on him for any cases involving drunk driving. I'm always happy to give students a pass when a fact pattern hits too close to home. I figure Charlie probably picked up a DUI in college. He stops by my office a few days later to fill me in on the real reason.

A few years before Charlie started law school, a drunk Marine had gotten behind the wheel, driven the wrong way down a freeway, and struck a car full of medical students. The crash killed two of the students, including Charlie's sister. It is an agonizing story—lives lost, families shattered, dreams destroyed. The drunk Marine survived.

Charlie argued for leniency at the trial. He didn't see the fairness in sending the guy to jail for the rest of his life for an unintentional killing. There was plenty of heartache behind the scenes. Not all of his family agreed; not all of his friends understood. The judge sentenced the drunk Marine to the low end of a manslaughter conviction. Was that fair?

I receive my own lesson in fairness a few days after my discussion with Charlie. It is just after dinner, and I am due in court. I have thrown on a suit and tie to look as professional as possible, and I am carrying a case file with the relevant documents. As I pass through the metal detector, a security guard asks, "Attorney?"

"No," I answer softly. "Tonight I am here as the defendant."

I am in traffic court for the first time in my life. And I am terrified. When I was practicing law, I litigated cases, cross-examined witnesses, and made closing arguments. As a professor, I have taught future prosecutors, defense attorneys, and even judges. I know courtrooms.

But I don't know *this* courtroom.

This courtroom is far afield from the halls of justice I have seen on television shows or encountered in my own practice experience. There are no marble steps or majestic columns, no oversized doors, no statues of Lady Justice. Instead, the facade resembles a decrepit storefront at the end of a strip mall.

Inside, past the metal detector and guards, rows of folding chairs fill a large and otherwise open room. The prosecutor sits behind a nondescript plastic folding table on one side of the room. Across the room, the judge's plastic table is slightly fancier, elevated by a pair of risers and with the court's seal affixed to its front. But mostly I just see people sitting in rows and rows of folding chairs, waiting for their number to be called. This is the reality of many courtrooms in America.

I got the ticket for allegedly turning right on red at an intersection with a "No Right on Red" sign. I have an explanation of course. The traffic signal was terribly confusing, with alternating flashing and solid yellow lights. In the midst of all this confusing yellow, how was I supposed to know the next signal would be red and not green? Officer Sniderman was not interested in my explanation.

Lauren, my sixteen-year-old, was with me in the car. She immediately pulled out her phone and started texting.

"Are you texting your friends that I just got pulled over?"

"No, Dad. Why would I do that?"

I don't know. I'm just making small talk so I don't start cussing in front of you.

In addition to managing my complex emotions in front of Lauren, I also realized after-the-fact that I felt no concern for our safety as Officer Sniderman approached our car. No concern about reaching into my glove compartment for my registration. No concern about where my hands were at any given time or where Lauren put her hands when she pulled out her phone. No concern when I rolled my eyes after Officer Sniderman asked me if I was in a hurry. I've heard enough stories from friends to know this is not everyone's experience.

The back of my ticket reads, "YOUR FAILURE TO APPEAR IN COURT AT THE TIME SPECIFIED OR OTHERWISE RESPOND TO THE CITATION AS DIRECTED MAY RESULT IN THE SUSPENSION OF YOUR DRIVER'S LICENSE AND MAY RESULT IN A WARRANT BEING ISSUED FOR YOUR ARREST."

This sounds serious. I thought about just paying the fine. But Officer Sniderman had handed me an "instruction sheet" along with the ticket, which contained this sentence: "If your violation is not listed on this sheet, you must appear on the court date specified." And turning right on red was not listed on the sheet.

I had no idea what to do, so I called a lawyer. After listening to me describe my situation, she told me she could take my case. But she also asked, "Aren't you a lawyer?" And she suggested I just go to court and talk to the prosecutor.

So here I am on a Tuesday night, having taught my Criminal Law class just a few hours earlier and now finding myself as the criminal defendant, walking up to the row of chairs in front of the prosecutor's plastic table. I had debated about whether to put on the suit, but now I'm glad I did, because the prosecutor is dressed for business. The suit also makes me sweat more than usual, and the large room starts to feel stuffy and small.

The prosecutor calls the man in front of me, who is not dressed for business. I am within earshot of their conversation and learn he is here for a speeding ticket. He is very sorry, but he thinks the officer clocked him faster than he was actually driving. He and the prosecutor chat for a bit longer, and she tells him she is going to reduce the charge. She asks him if he has brought a form of payment. He has not. "Okay, I am just going to dismiss this ticket. You are free to go. Have a great day."

The man's face lights up as he turns to leave. Then it's my turn. I walk up to the prosecutor and open my file.

She looks up and greets me: "Hi, how can I help you?"

"Hello . . . I'm, I'm . . . I'm here for a traffic ticket," I stammer. And then, before she can respond, I blurt out, "I called a lawyer, but she told me that since I'm a lawyer, I should just come talk to you."

I begin to slide my file over to her but pull it back when I worry she might think I'm slipping her a bribe.

"You're a lawyer?"

"Yes. But I really have no idea what I'm doing right now."

The prosecutor smirks at my self-evident commentary and then pulls my file closer to glance at it. "Why were you turning right on red?"

My first instinct is to plead the Fifth. Maybe this is a trap. What kind of lawyer-defendant would just answer the prosecutor's question, especially one so clearly tailored to elicit an admission of guilt? Then I remember this is traffic court and invoking my Fifth Amendment right against self-incrimination would look awfully pretentious.

"Well, you see, there was this flashing yellow light—"

"Oh, whatever," she interrupts. "I am going to dismiss this ticket. Have a nice day."

As I get up to walk away, she adds, "By the way, nice job bringing a file. Nobody does that."

I am elated. I want to jump up and dance or reach over to hug the prosecutor. But it also occurs to me that power and privilege have walked with me through every step of my alleged right-on-red violation.

I comfort myself a little by remembering that the prosecutor also dismissed the ticket of the man who went before me, and he wasn't wearing a suit or carrying a file. Maybe she was just in a good mood tonight. But that doesn't make this process fair—it just means this man and I both lucked out together. Maybe tomorrow's docket won't be so lucky.

As I reflect on the overall experience of my ticket, these questions of fairness only grow louder. Some people have their lives upended in similar circumstances. They don't get their tickets dismissed, can't pay the fines, have warrants issued for their arrest. Some people go to jail for traffic offenses. Some people don't get to reach for their registration or roll their eyes without fearing—or facing—dire consequences.

This reminds me of an experience I had a few years earlier. I was visiting a friend, a very accomplished law professor at Duke. It was during the summer, and we were both dressed casually, wearing T-shirts and jeans. As I dropped him off in front of his school after lunch, I pulled into a waiting area while we finished our conversation. The sign in the waiting area read, "Ten-minute parking for pick-ups and drop-offs." Within a few seconds, a campus police officer pulled alongside and motioned in our direction. "You all are leaving now, right?"

I turned to the officer and rolled my eyes at him—I have a terrible poker face, especially when I'm annoyed and, apparently, especially with police officers. I was about to tell him to come back and ask us that question again in nine minutes and thirty seconds. But in the time it took me to turn to the officer, my friend was extending his hands in front of him, palms up. "No problem, Officer. I'm reaching to open the door and leaving right now." And he opened the door, exited the car, and walked away.

I was fuming as I drove off and called my friend a few minutes later. "Why did you let that cop push you around? You could have called Duke's president and had that guy fired."

My friend, who is black, calmly responded, "The fact that you would even ask that question means you still don't understand. That guy has two categories for people who look like me—custodial worker and trespasser. If we had been off campus, a police officer would have had to think twice about a black man, since I might be a businessman or a politician. But not on campus. And that guy had a gun."

All of this had gone through my friend's mind in the few seconds it took me to turn toward the officer and roll my eyes. On that campus, and in our profession, my friend held a lot of power and prestige. But in that moment, he knew his power and prestige meant nothing. And that is always his reality and never mine. And that doesn't seem very fair.

Sometimes it is easier to tell what's fair. Like determining who gets The Seat in our faculty meeting.

The faculty meeting is one of the strangest rituals of academic life. It occasionally has a purpose, like when we need to vote on a new hire or approve the curriculum. But most of the time, it's like wedding planning, expanding to fill whatever time it's allotted. Law faculty meetings are especially tedious

because everyone there is a lawyer. Imagine forty lawyers
debating the finer points of *Robert's Rules of Order* before
voting on the color of the new carpet for the faculty lounge.
At least practicing lawyers know that inefficient meetings cost
them billable hours.

The Seat is farthest back on the left side of the faculty
meeting room, a mostly windowless but brightly lit space large
enough to fit the whole faculty and a handful of administrators.
The tabletops are configured in a U-shape, apparently so
we can all look at each other during our meetings. The Seat
uniquely rewards its occupant with a bit of distance from
others in the room and the freedom to discreetly read emails.

Brenda and I are always in competition for The Seat, and
this adds a sliver of excitement to days with faculty meetings.
Whichever one of us arrives first makes a point of gloating to
the other across the room. One time, Brenda tried to claim
The Seat with a sticky note she placed on it earlier in the day.
But I just ignored the note and sat down anyway. Saving seats
is not in *Robert's Rules of Order*. Brenda should know that; she's
a lawyer.

Today I beat Brenda, which allows me to disappear into the
world of my email, paying only minimal attention to the report
from the curriculum committee. But twenty minutes later, my
ears perk up when the dean mentions an upcoming review of
the school's free speech policy.

The current policy commits to the "open exchange of ideas
and information" and insists that all members of our school
"respect the expression of ideas, even those that are offensive
or unpopular." It sounds good on paper, but the applications
are always messier than the theory. This week's review had

been prompted by an incident on the anniversary of 9/11. The College Republicans had set up tiny American flags around the perimeter of the main campus quad to commemorate the lives that had been lost that day.

A few hours later, a Muslim student began removing all of the flags and stuffing them into large trash bags. The student wanted to collect the flags to protest the tribute's patriotic focus—as he noted, not all of the victims were Americans. And he wanted to draw attention to the hundreds of thousands of deaths in the ensuing war in Iraq—a war based on faulty intelligence about weapons of mass destruction and tenuous links to al-Qaeda. One of the College Republicans happened upon the student, took a video of the flag-removing activity, and posted it online. And then the conservative media had a field day. Some of the online rhetoric included awful and threatening words toward the protester, and someone posted his name and address online. The ensuing discussion around campus was what should happen to the student who took down the flags.

As the faculty discussion begins, Brenda suggests that the only viable option is to focus on procedure rather than substance. Because our school lacks a clear concept of "justice," we won't be able to say whether or how free speech serves justice. But we *can* set up rules of engagement that everyone has to follow—we can require procedural fairness. We can have rules about who can make public expressions and when they can make them, and we can have rules governing protests against that expression. But all of this is quite different from arbitrating whether actions are fairly punished or rewarded relative to our understanding of what is good or right. Without specifying what our school actually believes about the world, we can't do much more than require people to follow the procedures.

A few of my colleagues jump into the discussion, some building on Brenda's observations, some pushing back, and others making largely unrelated points. After glancing at the clock in the back of the room, the dean tells us we will have to resume the conversation down the road. The meeting ends after a few less exciting updates. I surrender The Seat and walk out of the building with Gary Richardson.

Gary is in his fifth year on the faculty. He's a legal historian who focuses on the Fourteenth Amendment—one of the immensely important reconstruction amendments that has shaped debates around liberty and equality in our country— debates about fairness. Gary is a white guy from Iowa who grew up below the poverty line in a single-parent home. He was the first in his family to attend college. After excelling in high school, he earned a full ride to Iowa State and flourished there with the help of a few mentors in the history department who saw his brilliance and aptitude. Harvard was the easy part. He spent seven years completing his JD and PhD. Sure, everyone at Harvard was just as smart as he was. But not everyone had labored as hard to get there. While in high school, Gary had worked construction during the summers to cover some of his mom's medical expenses, and then he had worked the night shift at Target every semester at Iowa State to pay for books and housing.

Gary and I usually meet after the faculty meeting. We try to walk when the weather is nice, but today it's raining. So we decide instead to meet at Whispers, the campus coffee shop in the undergraduate library. I suppose some administrator thought Whispers was a clever name for a coffee shop attached to a library. But the students find it worthy of mocking. *Meet me at Whispers. Crazy night at Whispers. What happens at Whispers stays at Whispers.*

After making my way to Whispers with a cheap and largely ineffective umbrella that I should probably replace, I splurge on a mocha and oversized cookie. Gary sticks with coffee. After we sit down, I begin venting about the protest discussion we've just had in the faculty meeting.

"Brenda is right. The reason we default to procedural rules in every fraught situation is that we have no sense of what we actually care about," I begin. "We don't know what we value as an institution because we don't know our purpose. And without knowing what we value, we can't really decide what's fair."

Gary pushes back. "We can approximate fairness without naming a specific purpose. Some institutions never know their purpose, while others have many different purposes. They can still make judgments about fairness."

"Maybe that's true. But wouldn't it be better for schools like ours to be clear about our purpose? Like teaching students how to be lawyers?"

"Doesn't that mean teaching them about procedural fairness?"

I pause for a few seconds, wondering if he may be right.

"No, I think it's more than that."

I suggest to Gary that even proceduralism aspiring toward fairness can still be fundamentally unfair. Think about a judge who imprisons a single mom because she failed to pay her court fees. That may be procedurally fair, but that doesn't mean it's good or right. Knowing what is good or right means knowing purpose and values. And just as the criminal law doesn't always explain its purpose in punishing unpaid court fees—or how it punishes unintentional homicides—our law school rarely pauses to examine its underlying purpose. I tell Gary I wish we had more coherence.

"Coherence?" Gary asks skeptically. "People and the institutions they create are too messy for coherence. I'll settle for functionality."

Maybe he's right. But I worry that functionality without clarity around our values means we will never get to the questions that really matter. Procedures and rules won't answer our hardest questions about fairness—questions like those about how to punish the drunk Marine. Nor can we resolve questions of fairness through appeals to intuition. When we are left to our own devices, our sense of fairness emerges out of our own stories and experiences. Most of us tend to think our intuition is right more often than not.

But when you think about it, not all questions of fairness are unanswerable. Sometimes procedural fairness can go a long way. We could agree on how much time people should speak in class or decide that I should always get The Seat at faculty meetings. Maybe Gary is right that procedural fairness is the best approach to our campus free-speech clashes.

We can also move beyond procedural fairness to more complicated questions of substantive fairness. For example, we can ask what may be unfair about the criminal justice system, from traffic stops to incarceration, regardless of whether we personally experience this unfairness. Just because we won't ever make the world perfectly just and fair doesn't mean we can't strive to make it fairer and more just.

What Happens When **We Can't Compromise?**

Life is a zero-sum game.

George Carlin

By mid-October, the trees are starting to lose their foliage. And this means that some weekends I am raking a lot of leaves. On this particular Sunday afternoon, my kids pretend to help. But mostly they are fixated on the pile I have made, which is just large enough to cushion their acrobatic landings. Lauren has become uncannily good at recording slow-motion videos, which makes the leaves exploding upon Sam's impact seem even more dramatic. Hana, my middle child, is laughing on the side and definitely not helping me rake. Of course, their frolicking means more raking for me, but I decide I'm okay with this particular trade-off.

At work the next day, I'm annoyed when I glance at the clock on my computer. I've forgotten about this month's faculty meeting, and it starts in five minutes. There goes my afternoon plan to do some reading. More importantly, I know I have already lost The Seat to Brenda.

I hurry down to the faculty meeting with the brisk walk, one of the many unheralded soft skills required of a professor. Faculty like me perpetually cram too many meetings and appointments into a day already busy with classes. But when we're trying to get from one place to another, we can't move so fast that we embarrass ourselves scampering past our students like Ed Rooney in *Ferris Bueller's Day Off*. The brisk walk strikes the right balance. Not too fast to break a sweat, but purposeful enough to signal that I don't have time for more than a passing hello. Of course, the brisk walk is best left to the workplace. Sometimes I forget when I am out with my family and absentmindedly begin outpacing them for no apparent reason. This has caused Hana to ask on more than one occasion, "Why are you like this?" It's a good reminder that efficiency and presence are sometimes mutually exclusive.

I arrive just in time for the start of the faculty meeting and studiously avoid making eye contact with Brenda, who is no doubt gloating across the room. Today we are talking about upcoming hiring needs, and I already know where this discussion is headed. Faculty hiring brings out unpleasant tensions even among relatively congenial colleagues like mine. That's because these decisions are usually zero-sum. We have a limited number of positions, and we can only check so many boxes with any particular hire. There's not a lot of room for compromise.

The dean begins by saying he wants to give the faculty great latitude to hire in whatever areas we think are most needed. But he reminds us of a few things. We haven't hired anyone in national security law in quite some time. We have strengths in employment law that we could build on. We have holes in the first-year curriculum, especially property. It would be nice to have someone who does oil and gas. And don't forget about diversity.

Bill Collins, our resident national security expert, speaks first. "I have to agree with the dean that it would be good to have someone else doing national security law. I can't hold down the fort forever." I think to myself that if anyone is going to test the limits of forever, it's going to be Bill, who, as legend has it, started here sometime during the Truman administration.

Jackie Davison, an employment law scholar, weighs in to let us know that this is the right moment to build on our employment law strengths.

The faculty who teach property all chime in about our property needs.

Since nobody does oil and gas, that one goes unmentioned. A few people make known their diversity preferences.

I decide to jump in and make a pitch for more half-Japanese First Amendment scholars. Being both half-Japanese and a First Amendment scholar, this feels like an appropriate interjection in light of the discussion that has been unfolding. Judging by the ensuing silence, my colleagues underappreciate my joke. The dean ends this portion of the meeting promising to take all of these thoughtful perspectives under consideration. And truthfully, all of them have some merit. But in a world of limited resources, we can't satisfy everyone's preferences. Compromise is not always possible.

Criminal law is full of situations where compromise is not possible—guilt or innocence, life or death, prison or parole. Prosecutors and defense attorneys avoid or obscure some of these stark choices through plea bargaining and other negotiation tactics. At some point, however, certain zero-sum decisions are unavoidable. Monday's class introduces another example when compromise isn't possible—self-defense.

In most self-defense cases, the killer is either guilty

of murder or not guilty of any offense because they acted reasonably; for example, they reasonably believed that the person they killed was about to kill them. But figuring out what is reasonable is not self-evident, and it depends on what the law says. Part of the reason George Zimmerman was acquitted in 2013 after shooting and killing an unarmed Trayvon Martin was that Florida's "stand your ground" law created layers of substantive and procedural protections for someone in Zimmerman's situation. That doesn't make Zimmerman's actions reasonable to the average person, but it made them *legally* reasonable. And the outcome is zero-sum. Zimmerman's acquittal means that Trayvon Martin's death was not a murder in the eyes of the law.

These questions about self-defense are further complicated when we turn to domestic abuse. The key case involves Judy Norman, a woman who faces unspeakable mental, physical, and sexual abuse from her husband, J.T. Take my word for it, J.T. is a monster. He spends twenty years abusing Judy in every possible way. And after that long, Judy can't bring herself to flee. J.T. has an emotional hold on her. But Judy is also convinced J.T. is going to kill her in one of his fits of rage, and she is probably right. One hot summer night in June 1985, as J.T. is sleeping, Judy puts a gun to his head and pulls the trigger.

Did Judy act in self-defense?

This is an awful thought experiment for my students. There is no way Judy meets the legal standard of reasonably fearing imminent deadly harm. J.T. was asleep. But day after day, he has been beating Judy and forcing her to do all kinds of vile things. What should she have done?

"What would *you* have done?" I ask a somewhat startled Joe Villario, the Navy officer I met at orientation who has ended up in my class. Even as I ask the question, I wonder to myself whether anyone can really say what they would have done without having lived Judy's life of trauma and fear at the hands of J.T.

Villario thinks for a minute and then says, "I would have pulled the trigger. She had no other choice."

The judge sentenced Judy to six years for manslaughter, and the governor commuted her sentence. Maybe that's a fair outcome. But it's also kind of a cheat. Judy intentionally killed J.T. in the absence of an imminent threat. Either she is a murderer or she's not—there is no middle ground. There is no compromise.

After class, I drive to the airport for a quick trip to Minneapolis to present a paper at the University of Minnesota. My plane out is mostly empty, and the flight is uneventful—I pass the time watching *The Office* on the in-flight entertainment. I arrive in downtown Minneapolis early enough to spend a few hours strolling up and down the part of Nicollet Avenue that feels like an outdoor mall. After I present my paper, some faculty members and I head to dinner, and then I settle into my hotel.

My return flight the next morning is completely full, and I find myself sitting next to a woman with a large dog crammed into a little dog suitcase. The dog is yelping, despite its owner's frantic attempts to quiet it.

I get that people like their pets. And the travel industry would like to accommodate those people and their dollars. But what about people like me who are allergic to the pets? My allergies are severe enough that I take regular allergy shots. The shots are not completely effective, which means I still have to be relatively careful around the plants, dust, and animals I encounter in the world. This reality leads to a mix of frustration and befuddlement whenever I discover that my airplane seatmate has a furry little companion.

It happens more frequently than you might think. My dog-carrying seatmate inevitably opens up a little flap in the carry-on suitcase, which means the dog and I are breathing the same air and my eyes are watering and my nose is running. Something similar happens in "pet-friendly" hotels, even the ones that advertise "pet-free" rooms, as if the hotel's HVAC system will magically filter out the allergens from my room or the $150 cleaning fee charged to the room's previous pet-friendly occupant will really ensure the room is cleared of dog hair.

There are a few ways to think about this problem of pet lovers and allergy sufferers. One of them, which I assume the travel industry relies on, is to figure out who is willing to pay more. Let's say it's worth $20 to my seatmate to have Fluffy with her on the plane and it's only worth $15 for me not to have my eyes watering when Fluffy is next to me. The challenge is figuring out how we would know. Perhaps the airlines could ask everyone to pay and see who pays more. But the airlines aren't going to ask for individual preferences; they care about aggregate preferences. So maybe it really comes down to who has the bigger market share—the dog owners willing to pay to have the dogs or the people with allergies willing to pay not to have the dogs. Judging by the number of times I have sat next to a dog, it appears the airlines have concluded it's the former.

On the other hand, the allergy sufferers don't always lose. These days, if someone on a flight has a peanut allergy, the flight attendant usually announces that they won't be serving peanuts. But what if I really like peanuts and have even paid extra to fly with this airline because they have really good peanuts? It's not obvious why we should feel differently about peanuts than we do about dogs—in both cases, some people have experienced life-threatening allergic reactions.

Nor are peanuts and dogs the only zero-sum airline challenges. Think about the guy who reclines his seat back into your lap after takeoff. How do we decide whether his right to recline beats your right to that precious bit of space in front of you? And we haven't even gotten to the middle seat armrests.

These airline examples point to a broader reality, namely, that our lives are full of clashing values and priorities not readily prone to compromise. In many instances, the law decides those clashes for us. Sometimes, perhaps often, these legal resolutions create a world that some people celebrate and others lament.

After my dog-filled flight lands, I head straight from the airport to my office for a few student meetings. Afterward, I stroll into Brenda's office to share my musings about airline policies. Some people returning from a trip might start the office chatter by recounting the people they met or the food they enjoyed. But we are law professors, which means we begin by discussing the allocation of rights and responsibilities in air travel.

Brenda suggests the difference between peanuts and dogs comes down to money. Someone has figured out that risk of litigation and bad publicity from the kid with the peanut allergy outweighs the cost of not accommodating the allergy. Nobody is going to sue you for not having peanuts on the plane. And the person who really wanted the peanuts probably isn't going to pick a different airline simply because they missed out on them.

My conversation with Brenda is well-timed before my next Criminal Law class, where I talk about the role of the law when we can't compromise. I want my students to grasp the significance of *how* the law decides for us. It's not through gentle persuasion. The uncomfortable truth is that the law anchors its authority to resolve otherwise irresolvable differences in its power to use violence.

Law students do not always like the idea that the law enforces its decisions with the threat or use of violence. Criminal Law class exposes this reality more starkly than some other classes, but the same lethal force underlies more seemingly mundane legal actions such as enforcing contracts and resolving property disputes. Most of us don't see this reality because most of us comply with legal norms. But try ignoring a key contract provision or deciding not to pay your rent or mortgage and see what happens. And then see what happens after you refuse to comply with the police officer who shows up to enforce your legally binding agreement. Actually, don't do that—just take my word that it won't go well for you.

The point is that lawyers, judges, politicians, and police officers do not interpret poetry; they interpret laws backed by coercive force. And their interpretations of these laws have consequences. I tell my students that if all they want to do is interpret texts, they should get a PhD in English. Every so often, one of my students who happens to have a PhD in English bristles at the comment. But most of my students get the point. The law is a *profession* because the stakes are high, and the rules of the game are codified and complex. Nobody cares about your personal opinions. They care about your arguments and how your arguments relate to the relevant legal issue. And sometimes when compromise isn't possible, your arguments mean that people live or die.

This message is not just for future prosecutors; it's also for the transactional lawyer in a fancy suit who spends most of their time helping rich people stay rich. That lawyer provides value to their client because they understand *the law*, which means they understand what other lawyers and judges are likely to say and do. And after the other lawyers and judges speak—especially the judges—their white-collar client making seven figures had better comply. If that client refuses, someone will call the police. And if the client ignores the police, they will eventually be met with violence. The law is violent because it is ultimately enforced with violence.

The future Wall Street lawyers do not always like this particular Criminal Law class. But I hope they remember it. I want them to understand that law rests on a kind of authority rooted in the threat of violence. I want them to wield power with the care that it deserves, whether from the prosecutor's table, the judge's bench, or the corporate boardroom. Because when law cannot resolve conflicts with compromise, it resolves them with force.

Not that I would want it to be otherwise. And neither would you. Think for a minute about the alternative—a world without law. A world where it's everyone for themselves and violence reigns unconstrained. A world with unending cycles of vengeance where the people with the most strength dominate and exploit the people who are most vulnerable. You might point out that this already happens anyway in a world governed by law. And you would be right. But think how much worse it would be if the law no longer constrained any of our worst impulses.

A world with law—the world we all prefer—means a world of winners and losers in politics, policies, and legal disputes. These clashes include smaller conflicts over pets and allergies and weightier ones such as those surrounding the abortion debate, the scope of religious freedom, and the right policy on gun ownership.

You may decide that some of your beliefs about these issues are not open to compromise. And sometimes you will find those beliefs on the losing end of a law or policy. In those moments when compromise isn't possible and you've lost, it's natural to feel like the whole system is rigged or needs to be reimagined. In practice, though, it's more pragmatic to keep fighting within our law-governed system rather than trying to destroy it. Trying to upend the system usually ends in futility, frustration, or chaos. Few people who don't already agree with a movement will be convinced by its calls for revolution. These kinds of rallying cries appeal to those whose views already lie in the extremes rather than to those who might be open to persuasion and political change.

When you find yourself on the losing end of a conflict that cannot be resolved through compromise, you don't need to throw in the towel or blow up the system. An inability to compromise is not always a dead end, and even zero-sum decisions can usually be reconsidered. Use the opportunity to deepen your understanding of what's at stake in a disagreement and why others see things differently. And recommit to work toward a different solution while continuing in your efforts to persuade others that your position is, in fact, the better one.

Can We Have **Difficult Conversations?**

If you start a conversation
with the assumption that you
are right or that you must win,
obviously it is difficult to talk.

Wendell Berry

By early November, my students have enough classes under their belts to discern the relevant law and facts of the cases we are reading. This greater ease with the materials allows us to explore more sensitive topics that introduce more complex class dynamics. This morning's Criminal Law class is one of those opportunities. It begins a three-day unit on sexual assault.

I have mixed feelings about teaching sexual assault. This unit is the most difficult sequence of classes I teach. And I am certain I have made mistakes over the years—phrasing a response unclearly, missing a critical nonverbal cue from a student, jumping too quickly from one topic to the next. There is a big debate among law professors about whether even to teach the topic. It's incredibly fraught, and unlike many of the offenses we cover, the odds are overwhelming that some of the students in the class have personal experiences with sexual assault. And yet the legal and policy questions are important and complex, and it wasn't too long ago that law schools glossed over sexual assault because our society paid little attention to the nature of the crime and its victims. If we can't wrestle with these kinds of questions in a law school classroom, I'm not sure where else we should expect to do so.

One of the many difficult issues with sexual assault is the legal analysis of consent. In order to build to the hard questions, I always begin with a case of clear nonconsent: an assailant who forcibly rapes a woman at knifepoint. Starting with that case allows me to lay the groundwork for the basic elements of the offense before turning to more complex matters.

Early in my career, I once opened the discussion of this case with a few remarks about the sensitive nature of the topic and then asked my students for their initial impressions. A redheaded guy in his late twenties was the first to speak: "She was dressed provocatively. I think she wanted it."

There were a few audible gasps. A woman sitting in the back row stood up and headed to the door. Mostly there was just silence.

I knew that my next words mattered. An unqualified rebuke would have obliterated the student in front of his peers. On the other hand, ignoring his out-of-bounds comment might implicitly validate it and signal to others in the class that it was just another view being bandied about in our little marketplace of ideas. All of this was immensely complicated by the backgrounds and experiences of the speaker and the hearers. And I had just a few seconds to respond before losing control of the class. I looked out at the roomful of faces staring back at me with various emotions, all of them quite serious.

"In this case, it is clear that consent is not an issue, and there is no indication that the victim was anything less than forcibly assaulted," I began. "We are talking about a violent rape in which the culpable mental state of the assailant is firmly established by the facts."

To be honest, I do not remember my exact words, but I think they were something along those lines. Meanwhile, I remember a flood of thoughts entering my mind: *Try to be direct and factual. Do not let your own emotions overcome you. Do not react solely to the temperature of the room.*

I don't mean to overstate the pressure. It wasn't like I was performing open heart surgery or storming a beachhead. But it was pressure nonetheless. And I think the exchange illustrates how challenging classroom teaching can be. We are not just dusting off lecture notes we wrote years ago; we are covering emotionally and intellectually complex ideas with a diverse group of students who have never before experienced this discussion, in this setting, with these people. What plays out is impossible to anticipate in advance.

This is one of the reasons I worry about the impulse to condemn people even for really insensitive and hurtful comments. The dialogues that unfold in law school classrooms—like those that take place in workplace break rooms, at neighborhood parties, and in coffee shops—are not scripted. Inevitably, when these conversations turn to sensitive or complex ideas, the tone or substance of spoken words will hit a nerve or touch an emotion. Some of these miscues are intentionally disruptive or mean-spirited. Others—even the egregious ones we want to condemn most quickly—are not meant to offend.

The benefit of the classroom is that it offers an extended conversation with the same group of people. That means that most of the time, we're able to follow up with questions or further dialogue when we encounter confusing or off-putting comments. The exchange about sexual assault was an especially difficult moment. But even then, I knew we had the rest of the semester to build on a framework that allowed for continuing the conversation. And the space between classes allowed me to meet with individual students to talk through what had transpired and how we could improve our classroom dialogue going forward.

Most of us have similar opportunities with our coworkers, neighbors, and acquaintances. When you have a challenging conversation with someone you know, you can usually find ways to follow up if you're willing to put in the time and effort. It's fine to say something in the moment to express your discomfort or disappointment. But instead of leaving the relationship in an awkward limbo, take advantage of your proximity and familiarity to learn more rather than assume the worst.

Thankfully, the unit on sexual assault is uneventful this time around. After we finish those three class periods, we turn to a section of the course on attempt crimes, and before long, we are approaching Thanksgiving.

The days before Thanksgiving are usually filled with restless anticipation. In the last class before the break, I always tell my first-year students to be careful at the dinner table when they go home. Nobody wants to hear all the fancy words you have learned or why Mom's offer to pass the mashed potatoes is an implied contract or why Uncle Frank's view of the Constitution is wrong. Nobody cares. They care about you; they are glad you're learning new things; and they are really glad to see you. And please pass the mashed potatoes.

Of course, these days the Thanksgiving dinner table

for many people is far more fraught than navigating socially awkward law students. Many of us will encounter friends and relatives over the holidays who hold differing and increasingly emotionally charged beliefs about issues like immigration, mass incarceration, vaccine mandates, affirmative action, and the Middle East. There's a long list, and it's getting longer.

One way to navigate these encounters is by recognizing the limits to our own knowledge and understanding and embracing the likelihood that we won't be able to convince everyone who thinks differently than us why we're right and they're wrong. That means sticking with conversations—and relationships—even when they get difficult. Be as charitable as possible, ask good follow-up questions, and try not to get offended too easily. As much as possible, distinguish people from the ideas they hold. Other people are human beings with whom you share many things in common. That doesn't mean you will always share—or even respect—their ideas.

On second thought, though, if you want to practice these postures in actual relationships, it's probably best not to start with family. There's something a bit too intimate about family that makes everything harder. Start with a friend or a neighbor and save the tough family conversation for later. If you struggle with political or religious differences in your family, spend Thanksgiving talking about football, turkey, or whatever else you still have in common—even if it's mostly memories.

I made the mistake of ignoring my own advice a few years ago. The details aren't important. Or maybe they are deeply important, but I am not going to share them with you. Things did not end well, and my dad and I stopped talking to each other for a long time.

We were talking again a few Thanksgivings later. Dad had been diagnosed with lung cancer, and we were getting close to the end. There were no direct flights to Colorado Springs, so our family flew to Denver, rented a car, and got caught in a blizzard on I-25. When we finally made it to my parents' home, Dad was weaker and slower than I had ever seen him.

He was also happier than I had ever seen him—exuding gratitude, presence, and joy rather than retreating to the back room to play solitaire as he had done in years past. He was in immense pain, but he hid it well. My kids saw very little of the pain—they just saw Grandpoppy delighted to see them and not playing solitaire. Late at night, after my kids were asleep, his coughing would get worse. And a few months later, he had lost the energy to cough.

A lung cancer diagnosis usually means learning you are going to die sooner than you expected. But before my dad got sick, I had not realized that this particular diagnosis also tells you *how* you are going to die. It's not the serene passing away in the middle of the night that one hopes for. Those last few months of Dad's life were some of the hardest of my own. But I also learned a lot as I watched him die. I learned that sometimes you have to start talking again—even about hard things. And I learned that you can say things more gracefully and more honestly when you realize how few opportunities you have left to say them.

This year, we stay home for Thanksgiving, which means no airports or blizzards and more free time. Our family is hosting a few of the international students, which we have done a few times when we haven't traveled for the holiday. The students are excited to experience a "real American Thanksgiving," and we don't have the heart to tell them we just picked up a precooked turkey and the reason there is no pumpkin pie is that nobody in our family really likes it. But the students don't seem to care—they're just happy to be with us. And they get a kick out of Sam telling me, "You're a terrible, terrible parent," when I summarily deny his request for special Thanksgiving screen time.

Later that day, the Thanksgiving church service—yes, we Presbyterians really have those—is a bit of a mixed bag. I appreciate the sermon on gratitude, but when I wander down to the fellowship hall after the service, I overhear my friend Jack Cunningham griping about "the liberals" trying to take away the true meaning of Thanksgiving.

Jack is a retired banker in his late sixties with a standing Saturday morning tee time at the local country club. He's a nice guy, and he has hosted me for a few rounds at the club. Jack is also understated in his own sort of way. He has a lot of money but isn't flashy about it, country club notwithstanding. Rumor has it that he funds half the annual budget for the local homeless shelter, but he has never said a word about it. And Jack and his wife, Cindy, have taught the little kids in Sunday school for as long as anyone can remember.

I don't know the name of the man talking to Jack, though I recognize him vaguely. He looks to be about Jack's age—maybe older. And like Jack, he is dressed in a blue suit, which makes me think I should have at least thrown on a tie for the service.

I am within earshot as Jack lays out his thesis. "The Pilgrims may not have been angels, but we owe them a lot and it's fine to celebrate them. The liberals are destroying our heritage."

"We are heading toward socialism," says the man standing next to him.

I usually enjoy talking with Jack, but I am not eager to engage in this conversation. I just came over to grab a second cookie from the snack table. Still, I find myself listening in as Jack and his friend continue.

"It's all because of critical race theory," I hear Jack whisper under his breath.

When I studied critical race theory years ago in graduate school, I found much of it enlightening and some of it bizarre. But it was all fairly complicated, the kind of thing one talks about in graduate school seminars and not, for example, in the fellowship hall after the Thanksgiving church service.

The simplest way I can describe critical race theory is that it is a method of questioning the assumptions behind different cultural baselines. *Why for so many years did we read mostly dead white guys in the standard English literature canon? Why did vagrancy and loitering laws emerge in many Southern states? Why are most churches racially segregated?* These critiques contend that power—and sometimes state-sanctioned law and policy—is behind the cultural baselines that some of us take for granted. And they seek to expose and weaken those uses of power.

I find this approach often helpful and sometimes necessary when it comes to understanding race and related critiques based on gender and other categories. It's good that we now consider the "reasonable person" rather than the "reasonable man" in evaluating the nature of resistance in sexual assault cases. It's good that we are reading more diverse perspectives into humanistic disciplines. It's good that we understand the massive racial disparities underlying criminal policy and sentencing.

At the same time, I've always thought that critical theory works best when it has something to critique. So when the English department assigns a canon of mostly dead white guys, I think it is helpful to have some sessions or even entire courses critiquing the canon from feminist, racial, and other perspectives. I'm glad when the canon is disrupted and reimagined. But I start to lose sympathy when critical theory *becomes* the canon. It is useful to point out Augustine's misogyny or Martin Luther's antisemitism; it is not useful to envision learning theology or political theory without Augustine or Luther, or entirely through a bunch of critical theory courses.

It also occurs to me that our mostly white church might reasonably be subject to some of the critiques of critical race theory. It's never a good sign of racial diversity when the half-Japanese guy is the only one adding color to the room. I grew up in churches like this one, and I find a lot that is comfortably familiar and spiritually invigorating. But the older I get, the more I realize how everything about these churches reflects a culturally white baseline—the sermon topics, worship style, rhythm, structure, tone, lament, and prayer. It's not like any of it is self-conscious. We don't think of the pastor as the "white pastor," the musician as the "white musician," or the church as the "white church." To us, it's just "church." But it's like what David Foster Wallace says about a fish's sense of water: the most important realities are sometimes the hardest ones to see. Especially from the inside.

On the other hand, the certainty and sanctimony of those who relentlessly excoriate the Jack Cunninghams of the world don't help. Words and phrases like *white supremacy* and *white fragility* often enter discussions and social media posts without context or explanation, when the point is often more to condemn than to persuade. As with any belief, recent converts are often the most zealous. The white person who grew up oblivious to these ideas reads a few books or attends a few lectures and suddenly feels compelled to evangelize. And it's often a fairly uncharitable evangelism. You may have seen this in some of your own social circles.

Maybe a reasonable place to start is to recognize that generations of redlining and other forms of housing discrimination, discriminatory lending practices, and even the legal status of churches have benefited white churches even as they have harmed black ones. That doesn't mean everything white churches do is bad, and it doesn't legitimize every critique of them. But it should mean an openness to critique and a willingness to change when we have fallen short.

Part of me wants to share these thoughts with Jack and his friend, but I decide that, like the Thanksgiving family dinner, this isn't the right time. Difficult conversations aren't cost-free, and I don't want to incur those costs today. Plus, if I am honest with myself, I have less patience for these kinds of conversations than I do for my classroom exchanges with students. I think it's because I have constructed a false dichotomy that characterizes the classroom as a learning environment where people discover new ideas and perspectives and sometimes make mistakes as they try them out—as if the rest of life weren't that too.

I sneak that second cookie while avoiding eye contact with Jack and walk back over to my family.

I think for a few days about writing an opinion piece about Presbyterians and critical race theory but ultimately decide against it. I just don't have enough emotional bandwidth right now. I like writing because it helps me figure out what I think. But I have learned that whenever I write something public that touches nerves, I need to carve out space to deal with the negative reactions. Not all comments are conversations in the making.

A few years ago, I wrote a piece titled "How to Unite in Spite of Trump." Something for everyone, right? Well, sort of. Here is a smattering of the responses:

> **Peter M.:** *"Thank you for the hilarious rant. Academics like you walk tall in the corridors of power around the world so you have a large responsibility for creating stupid government. Please feel free to emigrate to the EU Utopia. I would be happy to pay your (one-way) fare."*

CAN WE NEGOTIATE FOR A FIRST-CLASS TICKET?

> **Marques W.:** *"I will NEVER come together with racist accepters of sexual assault and pathological lying trump voters. And yes, I mean NEVER. Nor do I know of ANY progressive who ever would either."*

So you're saying there's a chance?

> **Sharon K.:** *"In my sixty-two years, I have seen American culture get progressively crazier and, relatedly, more tyrannical. Civil war may be necessary to set things right."*

Sharon, I do not recommend taking up arms.

> **Richard M.:** *"You are liable for spreading hate-filled, spurious material, for being a tool of a global oppression being charged for fraud, genocide, treason, and crimes against humanity. You are guilty of breaking the Constitution and international criminal laws, and you will be held to account."*

If you're sending me to the Hague, would you be willing to split the cost with Peter M. for an upgrade on my flight?

I know I should never read the comments section. I promise I don't. These are all people who took the time to look up my contact info and write me personal notes. Most came over email, but a few sent along their views using an old-fashioned envelope and stamp. And I don't even get the worst of them—I have colleagues who have received death threats for their opinion pieces.

I don't ever write back snarky retorts. I just imagine them in my head and then shove the notes into an office folder called "Crazy Stuff." Of course, if you ever send me one of these over-the-top responses, you are now on notice that I might quote you in a book.

Still, despite what we might sometimes think, the trolls are the exception, not the rule. Most people do not send death threats to opinion writers. Most people do not go out of their way to email insults to law professors. Most people do not lose all of their sensibilities on social media.

The truth is that you can have difficult conversations, with most people, most of the time. But you will need to pay attention to context. It's rarely a good idea to begin a relationship with a difficult conversation. Far better to start by finding common interests and shared experiences, or at least learning each other's names.

Think about your closest friends. You can usually risk difficult conversations with them because you have built a reserve of trust over the course of living life together. And if you reach a point with a close friend where you can no longer have hard conversations, then take the time to reset the relationship with an ordinary experience before jumping into a heated argument.

We *can* have difficult conversations, but context matters.

Can We See People
Instead of Problems?

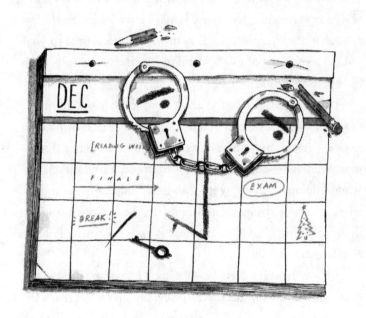

There are no ordinary people.

C. S. Lewis

On Tuesday morning, I am answering emails in my office when I hear a light knock at the door and look up to see one of my students, Jennifer Chang. I have forgotten that we are scheduled to meet, but I do my best to look unsurprised. Faking awareness of your calendar, like the brisk walk, is an indispensable professor skill.

Jennifer settles into the chair on the other side of my desk and pulls out a pen and a notepad. The first thing I notice is her posture. She is incredibly poised, better than most students—and much better than me. I find myself straightening up in my seat. Jennifer is half-Chinese and half-white. Before earning a philosophy degree at Brown, she went to one of those elite New England prep schools that I always conflate in my mind.

I know Jennifer vaguely—she took one of my classes last year. After a few minutes of catching me up on her plans for next summer, she asks if I will supervise her independent study. She is writing about Augustine and the place of gender-based legal distinctions in a democratic society. I always struggle with whether to accept these independent study requests. They are usually time-consuming and don't really fit naturally into my teaching rhythms. On the other hand, these projects sometimes allow for much deeper intellectual engagement than what is possible in the typical classroom setting.

I say yes to Jennifer's request, and we begin to discuss her project.

Thirty minutes into our meeting, I am regretting my decision.

"Jennifer, you have some great ideas, but you need to slow down and do some more background reading. You are jumping to conclusions about Augustine's arguments without having wrestled with what he's saying or the context in which he's writing."

"No, Professor, that's not the problem. The problem is that Augustine's misogyny fundamentally corrupts his views about citizenship."

"That's an assertion, not an argument. And it's not clear that you have read Augustine carefully, to say nothing of the secondary literature."

"Actually, I'm not sure you can understand the full implications of his misogyny, perhaps in part because you and Augustine are both men."

At this point, I'm inferring that a few classes at Brown have convinced Jennifer she has a duty to unmask all of the power structures that surround her. And apparently I am one of them. I look up at the clock and realize we are out of time.

"I'm sorry to cut short our discussion, but I have another meeting coming up, so let's talk again next week. In the meantime, please send me a three-page synopsis of your thesis."

Jennifer sends me her synopsis two days later. She is an exceptional writer, and she has already read some of the secondary literature I have suggested to her. But she has fallen into a typical student mistake of caricaturing arguments she dislikes.

We meet again the next week, and I spend some time unpacking the difference between advocacy and inquiry. Then I walk through a few specific suggestions and critiques. She nods along, maintaining her perfect posture. But her eyes make me think she's not really listening. We will have the next few months of meetings and revisions to see if I am right.

I have set aside the next day to visit the county records office. I have not stepped foot in that building since we moved here and I had to pay some kind of property tax. I have a vague recollection of where the office is located and a less vague recollection of never wanting to go back there. But now I need to return to search for a copy of an old property record. After I have spent ten years living in my house, my neighborhood association has decided that they own part of my yard.

This is just the kind of thing that neighborhood associations would waste their time on. The controversy stems from an easement, which falls on a strip of land in the back of our yard with a swing set, a fence, and a little fort I built for the kids one summer. The survey we received when we bought the house—the one the title company relied on to insure us—says we own the strip of land and have granted the association an easement to use the land if they ever decide to convert it into an alley. The association now says *they* own the strip of land and have granted *us* an easement. The county records office enters the story because neither the association nor I have copies of the actual easement, just a pile of other documents telling us it exists and that it is very, very old.

In the back of my mind, I think we are probably heading toward a lawsuit, which means I will have to hire a lawyer. Of course, I *am* a lawyer, but as every lawyer knows, it's usually a bad idea to represent yourself. Also, as you know, I had barely been able to resolve my traffic ticket, and this looks far more complicated. My dad was disappointed when he discovered that my undergraduate engineering degree did not mean I could fix the family television. I imagine if he were still around, he would be equally dispirited to learn that my law degree did not equip me to defend the family homestead.

The county records office is at the far end of a massive parking lot that appears to have every spot reserved for cars nowhere in sight. After circling the lot twice just to make sure I have not missed a nonreserved spot, I pull onto an adjacent road for streetside parking that requires some app I don't have on my phone. Fifteen minutes later, I am reasonably confident that I have managed to pay for my parking on the app and walk across the giant empty parking lot. After I enter the building, I see two lines of people in front of me. One line has assembled in front of an opening marked "Window 1: Walk-ins and Payments." The other is before an opening marked "Window 2: Appointments and Nonpayment Matters." I quickly construct a 2 × 2 grid in my head and realize that these line descriptions pose a problem for me because I am a walk-in (Window 1) for a nonpayment matter (Window 2).

I feel a pit forming in my stomach from this blend of inefficiency and ambiguity. I check the walls for any information that might resolve my dilemma—nothing. I pull out my phone and check the website for clues—nothing. I glance up at the two lines and notice the walk-ins line is significantly longer than the appointments line. I conclude that "walk-ins" beats "nonpayment matters" and pick Window 1.

Twenty-five minutes later, I reach Window 1 and learn that I have guessed wrong. "Didn't you see the sign? Window 1 is only for payments, and you are here for a nonpayment matter." Over I go to the back of the line for Window 2, which of course by now has gotten longer. When I finally make it to the front of that line, I learn that, like Plato's cave, I am at the precipice of a new reality. The man at Window 2 hands me a number and points me down the hall to a previously unseen line in front of a previously unseen Window 13.

After a considerable wait, Window 13 calls my number. I have a brief conversation with the clerk and fork over the $3 search fee (payable only by check, of course). A few minutes later, she returns to the window and hands me a copy of the easement. I walk exuberantly back to my car and drive home.

It's the wrong easement.

The next morning, I find my way back to Window 13. Then comes the next layer of Plato's cave. It turns out that the easement I need is only available on "the tapes." The tapes are stored on the fourth floor, and it's going to take some time to locate them. The man at Window 13 tells me that "Ms. J." is the only person who can perform the search. He takes my number and tells me Ms. J. will give me a call. By this point, I am not confident I will be hearing from Ms. J. anytime soon.

Ms. J. calls within a few hours. She has located the easement. I hurry excitedly back to meet her at her office.

After two days of navigating the county records office, Ms. J. is not what I expect. She is dressed impeccably and smiles pleasantly as she walks up to me. "Let me tell you what I've done," she begins.

Ms. J. spends the next few minutes explaining the easement. "This page was too faint to read, so I inverted the copier image to make it legible. My job is to help you do your job, and you can't do your job if you can't read it." She turns to the next page. "This one didn't have all of the right information, so I located a different version of the document. No extra charge for that."

At this point, I'm thanking her profusely.

"It's no problem. I love doing this work. I love my job."

I thank her again, and as I turn to walk away, Ms. J. says, "You have my number now; just call me directly if you have any more questions or queries."

I wonder how many people, once they finally get to Ms. J. after navigating the front-office bureaucracy of the county records office, take out their frustration on her. I wonder how close I was to being one of those people. Sure, everything worked out fine with Ms. J., but what if she hadn't smiled when she walked up, or what if she had copied one of the pages incorrectly? Ms. J. still would have been the same person I met. But would I have acted the same?

I also wonder how many frustrated lawyers, witnesses, and family members find their way to Ms. J.'s counterparts in the criminal courthouse across the street from the county records office and take out their frustration on people just trying to do their jobs. I want my students to think about these questions, which is why I make them visit a criminal courtroom.

The assignment is simple: *Spend thirty minutes watching*

a local criminal proceeding and send me a paragraph reflecting on your experience. I deliberately omit any other details. What courthouse? *You decide.* How will we know if a criminal proceeding is happening? *Figure it out.* How do we get into the courthouse? *Let me know when you find out.* What should we wear? *Don't ask me.*

The object lesson usually runs as intended—a mixture of nerves, uncertainty, and anticipation, followed by heartfelt reflections. A few students use their reflection to complain about the assignment, but most are glad I have made them do it.

- "It was really hard to access case and docket information on the courthouse website. It took me hours to figure out how to find the daily dockets. When I finally found a hearing to attend, I arrived at the courthouse listed online only to find out I was at the wrong location. Fortunately, a kind security officer told me where to go. When I got to the right location, someone else helped me find the room. I can't help but think that if I was a defendant who needed to show up for a court appointment, it would be very easy to get lost or confused and end up being very late."
- "At one point, a court employee approached a group of handcuffed defendants with some paperwork. She talked them through the legal forms as if they were boilerplate she had seen a thousand times. One of the defendants asked, 'What was that statute again?' After hearing the woman repeat it, a quick surreptitious search on my phone revealed that it described the effect of pretrial incarceration on the length of a prison term. This statute would

never be interesting enough for us to talk about in class, and I will likely make it through three years of law school without ever hearing about it again. But for this defendant, the language of that statute governed whether the next night of his life would be spent free or imprisoned."

- "The judge arrived fifteen minutes late, while the defendants sat in the small courtroom listening to the audible chatter and laughter at the public defenders' table. The attorneys' conversation ranged from 'really needing cookies' to congratulating a colleague on a new job. Their levity contrasted with the blank stares of the defendants. I imagine the daily demands of public defense necessitate lightheartedness—it just felt a bit out of place in the courtroom."

The awkwardness of navigating a courthouse for the first time is good training for my students. They don't know if they can ask questions, check their phones, or chew gum. In a few years, many of them will encounter similarly byzantine rules, websites, and hallways in the courthouses where they will practice. And the stakes won't be an ungraded memo for my Criminal Law class. Instead, their professional obligations, personal reputations, and clients' fates will be on the line.

The awkwardness that my students experience is also a good reminder that human interactions and emotions underlie all of these depersonalized bureaucratic rituals. Lawyers who encounter these systems day after day too easily forget the extraordinary pressures on clients and witnesses unfamiliar with the legal system. The person on the other end of your hundredth witness prep is likely undergoing their first prep;

the defendant arriving for what is to you a routine pretrial proceeding may still be anxious or afraid.

If lawyers risk forgetting the humanity of their clients in the banality of the courtroom, professors risk forgetting the humanity of their students in the doldrums of grading. Most faculty will tell you that grading is their least favorite part of the job. And law faculty will gripe about it even more because we don't have teaching assistants, and we grade everything at once. This is because in most law school courses, the semester grade rests entirely on the final exam.

Having been both a law student and a law professor, I can assure you that this particular norm is far worse for students. What kind of educational institution would design classes with that much pressure on a single exam and no meaningful feedback? It's a broken system, but there is a massive collective action problem that incentivizes faculty to stick to the status quo. And this is why I find myself in the middle of December with eighty Criminal Law exams waiting to be graded. Even though I know the students have the worse end of this experience, I am not looking forward to my own.

I find grading works best in familiar environments. For me, it's The Mad Hatter, a coffee shop a few miles down the road from my in-laws in Durham, North Carolina. We are visiting for Christmas, and after hours in the car and a few minutes of hugs and hellos, it occurs to me that it's time to start grading.

The coffee is overpriced and the menu is limited, but there's something about The Mad Hatter that just feels right.

It is housed in the bones of an old auto repair store, with big bay windows that allow for plenty of sunlight. I can look up in any direction and stare out one of the windows, which proves helpful for pondering. And this is good, since my life involves a lot of pondering.

The other upside of The Mad Hatter is that I can camp out at a table for long stretches of time as long as I avoid eye contact with anyone else looking for a place to sit. Years ago, I wrote most of my dissertation here, and I perfected the art of nursing a single cup of coffee for five hours to justify the unbroken possession of my table. Today, I am fortunate enough to spot an open table in the corner, and I pull out my exams and get to work.

Grading law school essay exams is more art than science. The key is judgment. And judgment comes with experience. The first time I graded exams, I had little confidence in what I was doing. But after a few rounds, I started to get a feel. Eventually, I got pretty good at the feel. But it still takes a lot of time to do it right.

Here is one thing I can tell you about grading law exams: it is pretty easy to identify the best and the worst ones. Then there is a big cluster of the class that just did fine. I call it The Middle. At our law school, The Middle is pretty good. You are about average among a group of really smart people who got into a highly selective law school, almost all of whom are going to make really great lawyers. But nobody likes being in The Middle, especially if you have never been there before, which is the case with most really smart people who got into a highly selective law school. And so a bunch of students in The Middle angst and angle to find a way out.

Inevitably, a few of them will want to meet after the exam, hoping to squeeze out a few more points from the semester: *Surely you forgot to account for that brilliant answer I gave in class or misread my essay or forgot about all of my great questions during office hours.* These very earnest intuitions are almost never right. I know this to be true because I have seen The Middle year after year. And also because I was in The Middle when I was in law school.

Except in Civil Procedure. There I was in The Bottom. I still remember getting my grades that semester. Back then, you called a number to hear an automated report. I called back four times just to make sure I had heard correctly, hoping that the computer on the other end had misspoken.

The computer on the other end had not misspoken, and a few days later, I found myself standing outside my professor's office. I entered nervously and began to speak.

"Professor, I understand that I might not have knocked this one out of the park, but I don't know why I am so far below an average grade."

The professor, an older man who did not seem particularly interested in teaching at this point in his career, pulled out a copy of my exam and glanced at it for a couple of seconds.

"Well, I probably did screw you over a bit on this one, but I am sure you did better than you deserved in some other class. Don't worry, it all works out in the end."

I try to remember this encounter when I meet with my own students. Everyone wants to be treated kindly rather than dismissively—to be treated as a person. That's true of students; it is also true of teachers, restaurant servers, cashiers, police officers, and salespeople. We don't have to agree with or even like the people we encounter in our lives, but we can begin and end our daily interactions remembering that we are talking with other human beings.

Back at my in-laws', my wife, Caroline, and I get into a stupid fight about when we will shop for Christmas gifts for our kids. Most of our fights start over trivial issues and escalate to absurd levels. It's a good reminder of how easily even those we care about the most can start to feel like problems to solve rather than people to love.

Fortunately, my legal training includes its share of conflict resolution. Unfortunately, not all aspects of "thinking like a lawyer" translate to ordinary people skills. I have learned this the hard way over the course of life since law school, most often with Caroline's assistance. It turns out that critically analyzing the premise of every claim is not always the best strategy in an argument with your spouse.

One of my most memorable arguments with Caroline came when I was billing my time. I spent most of my legal practice working for the federal government, which has its share of problems but at least lacks the billable hour. But I had a brief stint tracking my time while working for a boutique litigation firm just after I finished graduate school. I needed the money to cover our mortgage and health insurance with our second child, Hana, on the way. The more I billed, the more money I made.

One Saturday morning, I had started billing hours when Caroline and I got into one of those fights that you know within the first few minutes is not going to resolve quickly. This particular relational miscue led to four hours of arguing. Just before lunch, after half-hearted apologies, followed by more arguing, followed by real apologies, we were finally through it.

And that is when I made the not insignificant blunder of forgetting that, despite the trappings of the billable hour, not all time is reducible to dollars. I looked over at Caroline and asked, "Do you realize how much money this argument just cost us?"

When I share this story with students, they look at me incredulously. Surely no grown man could be this stupid. Surely this didn't really happen. But I was, and it did.

One of my takeaways from my experience with Caroline is that life isn't all about efficiency. Thinking back to my time at the county records office, I realize that Ms. J. saw me as a person rather than a problem because she chose to prioritize people in her life. When I am honest with myself, I am not very much like her. Too often, I prioritize efficiency. People with problems become interruptions rather than opportunities. And I am now realizing that I have started to make this same mistake with Jennifer Chang. Rather than seeing an opportunity to help her with her project, I have started to see an unwanted interruption to my life.

If you're like me, one way to guard against the tendency of seeing problems before people is to remind yourself of the complexity of the people you come across in your daily life. Everyone you meet is far more than whatever impression you have formed in your brief encounter with them. Remind yourself that everyone is handling a lot more in life than what you see. Try asking a friendly question rather than making all of your impersonal relationships purely transactional. And even if the person across from you is not as kind as Ms. J., give them the benefit of the doubt rather than being too quick to take offense. These are not really lawyer skills; in fact, the billable hour and the drive for efficiency leave many lawyers deficient in these abilities. But the happiest lawyers I know—and the happiest people I know—have learned to attend to their daily interactions without ignoring or dismissing the people around them.

Can We
Trust Faith?

Now faith is confidence in what
we hope for and assurance
about what we do not see.

Hebrews 11:1

After a few weeks of grading and vacation, January marks the start of a new semester and a new class for me: Law and Religion. Unlike Criminal Law, this is an upper-level class filled with students who have at least a year of law school and a summer internship behind them. Everyone is past the fear of the cold calls, and everyone knows how to read a case.

Everyone also has some skin in the game when it comes to this class. For some of my students, it's more traditional religious faith; for others, it's faith in an ideology or faith in themselves. But everyone has faith in something—we all choose a path that rules out other possibilities and implicitly stakes our lives on one faith claim or another. Law and Religion is a semester-long experiment in navigating the legal, cultural, and personal implications of living in a world of these competing faith claims.

One of the challenges in this class is figuring out how and why the law distinguishes among different expressions of faith. To start us down this path, I always teach the same case on the first day. It's actually a criminal case of sorts, at least insofar as Judith Kuch appears to be headed to jail by the end of the opinion. But we read it for the questions it raises about religious faith.

Judith is an ordained minister in the Neo-American Church. The church is a small and relatively obscure denomination, with a nationwide membership of roughly twenty thousand people at the time of her indictment. Judith's pastoral role means that she counsels people in crisis, helps interpret the church's teachings, and navigates various liturgies around songs and symbols.

The Neo-American Church's main problem is its principal teaching that members should partake of certain "sacraments," namely, LSD and marijuana. As you probably know, these particular practices run afoul of federal drug laws, and Judith finds herself facing a federal prosecution. Her defense relies on the free exercise of religion. Judith claims that she and her fellow adherents use LSD and marijuana as part of their worship, and she argues this should exempt them from otherwise applicable drug laws.

Unfortunately for Judith, Judge Gerhard Gesell concludes otherwise. He is aided by some of the details of the Neo-American Church in the record before the court. The church's leaders are called "boo hoos," supervised by a "chief boo hoo." Judith is mid-level management, serving as the "primate of the Potomac" and supervising boo hoos in her region. The church's official songs are "Puff, the Magic Dragon" and "Row, Row, Row Your Boat." Its key symbol is the bottle opener, and its official motto is "Victory over Horseshit!"

Judge Gesell finds these details "helpful" in rejecting Judith's free exercise defense. He thinks the church's teachings are "full of goofy nonsense, contradictions, and irreverent expressions" and deems the religious attributes "obviously only for tactical purposes." And he is probably right. A few years ago, I ran across an old copy of the Boo Hoo Bible, and it is exactly what you are probably thinking it is in light of the descriptions I have just given. Plus, the feds are serious about their drug laws. Views about marijuana use may be in flux today, but there is no way Judith is getting a religious exemption for LSD. Judge Gesell rightly notes that the free exercise clause simply cannot protect all religious acts. And just to underscore the point, he rattles off some other no-gos, including infanticide, the killing of widows, and temple prostitution.

So in one sense, this case is an easy one. But I start the course here because it forces students to think a bit more deeply about complex questions of faith. For one thing, do you know which other religious traditions have teachings that could be described as "full of goofy nonsense, contradictions, and irreverent expressions"? All of them. And I say this as someone firmly committed to one of them. I just mean that from the outside, if you don't believe the stuff, it can all sound a bit strange. In the Christian story, a virgin had a baby, a man came back to life, and that same man is coming back again someday, riding in on a horse surrounded by singing angels. And Jews, Muslims, and other religious people all have their own stories and doctrines that are not readily understandable to those outside these traditions.

In fact, many of our most deeply held beliefs will seem incomprehensible to others—beliefs about what makes us good or bad, about what gives people dignity, about the meaning of life. These questions tug at our strongest commitments and our deepest intuitions. They make sense to us because they are how we make sense of our lives. But chances are that if we tried to justify them to a smart inquisitor who does not share our understanding of the world, we would not be able to fully articulate everything we believe to be true.

On Thursday afternoon, I am doing the brisk walk to a faculty workshop across campus. A new colleague in the philosophy department whom I have not yet met is presenting a paper. Today's workshop is run by the political theorists. I feel a kindred spirit with this group, having studied political theory in graduate school. One thing I love about the theorists is that they can raise thought experiments without settling on any answers, like pondering the state of nature or a world without war or a cost-free healthcare policy. These kinds of open-ended imaginative inquiries can encourage fresh thinking and new ways of seeing old problems. But they sometimes come at the expense of staying grounded in real people and circumstances. When we move from theory to law, cases and statutes require answers to otherwise irresolvable questions. That's not to say the answers are always satisfactory, but at least they are answers.

I usually enjoy academic workshops, but you can only get to the valuable part if you cut through the performative fluff. The dialogue usually takes more or less the same shape every time:

> **Tanya Mitchell:** *"This is an extraordinary paper. Thank you so much for writing it and for challenging us with these impressive ideas. I have a three-part question. . . ."*

Jeff Carpenter: *"I, too, thought this paper was wonderful and amazing. And not to pile on, but I'm going to build off Tanya's question."* (*Jeff's question usually turns out to be the same question that Tanya just asked, worded slightly differently to make it sound original.*)

Bill Collins: *"As you know, my primary expertise is national security law. I'm wondering about the national security implications of your paper."* (*The paper usually has nothing to do with national security.*)

Jackie Davison: *"Could you say a bit more about the payoff section of your paper and how it applies to recent Supreme Court decisions?"* (*Jackie typically has not read the paper but feels the need to ask a vaguely worded question anyway.*)

There are inevitably a few more along these lines. But it's not all performative. And if you listen carefully, most people have helpful critiques and suggestions.

Today's discussion jumps into some well-trodden ground about the boundaries of "reasonableness" in public discourse. Is it reasonable to rely on the opinions of others? Is it reasonable to rely on intuition? Is it reasonable to rely on religious beliefs?

This last question sets off Tanya Mitchell, the prickly linguist sitting next to me. Tanya launches into a rant about her cousin Jim, a Christian fundamentalist who rejects climate change. For all I know, Jim's worldview is exactly as she describes. But it's a curious anecdotal intervention in a theoretical discussion.

It gets worse. The sociologist sitting next to Tanya whose name I forget adds, "I just can't really think of any Christians who I respect intellectually."

No offense taken, I think to myself. *Also, it should be "whom,"* but of course I don't say this out loud.

"Well, I thought Aquinas was pretty smart," says Jeff Carpenter, the theorist across the room. I'm sure Aquinas would be flattered.

Someone else jumps in to defend the Christians. "I once heard a guy at Yale who was a Christian, and he was very thoughtful."

We're up to two, not counting Cousin Jim and yours truly. At this point, I feel like the workshop has become a caricature—the kind of liberal arts vignette that would have the producers at Fox News salivating.

I finally jump into the conversation, suggesting that perhaps there are a few other plausible intellectuals among the billions of professing Christians on the planet. A couple of people nod, as if to say, *Yeah, he's got a point.*

I can't say it was my smartest contribution in a workshop, but there is only so much that comes to mind at the point of exasperation.

Maybe you have encountered a similar situation—a time when you have walked into a conversation or a social context that you expect to be familiar only to leave feeling like you have just had a cross-cultural experience. Perhaps you adhere to a particular religion and discover that the people around you have no understanding of, or perhaps even animosity toward, your beliefs. Or maybe you are an atheist or agnostic who finds yourself in a room where everybody starts to pray or someone demeans nonbelievers. I don't have any tips for eliminating the awkwardness, but one way to engage a little more gracefully is to remind yourself that everyone has faith in something, and everyone doubts.

Two weeks into the new semester, my Law and Religion class turns to another controversial issue—the relationship between religion and patriotism. This class calls attention to the kinds of cultural symbols that sustain a national identity rooted in some semblance of religious belief. In the United States, most of this narrative flows out of a white Protestant baseline that set the cultural norms for much of our country's history. In the middle of the twentieth century, the Protestants creatively renamed the baseline our "Judeo-Christian" heritage to bring Jews into the story.

Along the way, most Protestants stopped hating Catholics, which meant that "Judeo-Christian" encompassed Catholics too. There have been modest efforts to expand the tent even further, but these days the framing of a shared religious ethic for most Republicans is still "Judeo-Christian," while Democrats appeal to a more nebulous "religious heritage." Almost every public figure, regardless of politics or religion, still says "God bless America" at the end of important speeches.

We take up a number of these historical developments in

the first part of the discussion. Then I introduce the highlight of this class—a video I show of Lee Greenwood's song "God Bless the USA." The chorus is memorable—you've probably heard it:

> *I'm proud to be an American*
> *Where at least I know I'm free*
> *And I won't forget the men who died*
> *Who gave that right to me*
> *And I'd gladly stand up next to you*
> *And defend her still today*
> *'Cause there ain't no doubt*
> *I love this land*
> *God Bless the USA.*

I tell my students that I am always torn about the song. I used to love it, especially when I heard it while serving in the military. I once heard it played by the Marine Corps Band on the White House lawn on the Fourth of July. That's got to be a patriotism turducken.

I'm okay with a healthy dose of patriotism. One of the proudest moments of my life was when my dad—a career Army officer—administered the oath of office to me when I was commissioned as a second lieutenant in the Air Force. I have spent a lot of time with service members, some of whom risk more in a day than most of us do in a lifetime.

Still, there is a part of American patriotism that feels off to me. The "God Bless the USA" video I show to my class—a fan cut, not the official video—reinforces the dissonance: *Opens with an eagle and a flag. Cuts to the Twin Towers exploding on 9/11 with an image of a kid praying above them. Cuts to cute white family dressed in denim. Lots of flags. Statue of Liberty. Twin Towers again. Saluting Marine. More flags. Flag-draped coffins. More troops. Iwo Jima. USA signs. People waving flags and holding hands. More troops.*

The video goes on like this for the whole song, and it is honestly a bit overwhelming every time I watch it. And it's not like I'm showing an obscure video—this version has been viewed more than thirty million times.

There is one particularly startling image in the video—a little boy and girl praying with an American flag in the background and the caption "Faith in America" underneath. This to me is the key image for the class because it suggests that the logic of the Judeo-Christians is doomed to one of two fundamental errors. On the one hand, "Faith in America" could mean that the story of this country is principally the story of Christians (and perhaps a few Judeos). In this account, America is a "Christian nation." That was never fully true, but our changing religious demographics mean it is definitely not true today. On the other hand, "Faith in America" could mean that the story of this country is really about maintaining a religious-like belief in the goodness of "America" in which the object of worship is not God, but country.

I suggest to my class that neither of these narratives is particularly healthy or plausible. I don't think of this nation as either the embodiment of my faith or the object of my worship. Honestly, I feel a healthy dose of skepticism about the nation, regardless of who happens to be in charge at any given moment.

On the other hand, if Lee Greenwood, the Marines, and praying children don't give us a healthy version of patriotism, is there a better way to think of and celebrate our national identity? We are going to need more than the Olympics and natural disaster responses to sustain our collective American identity. But will we need faith? And if so, faith in what?

We return to these issues of patriotism a few classes later when we take up the Jehovah's Witnesses. In the 1930s and 1940s, the Witnesses were not the soft-pedaling evangelists some of us have encountered at our doorsteps. Back then, they engaged in abrasive street preaching and untoward ridiculing of other faiths. They also staunchly refused to comport with the patriotism that infused a country at war. In response, they faced laws and regulations that routinely suppressed their civil liberties.

In 1940, the Supreme Court ruled that the children of the Jehovah's Witnesses could not refuse to pledge allegiance to the United States in public schools. The decision fueled an outbreak of violence against the Witnesses that included beatings and killings. In the meantime, the Witnesses tried again. They made clear they were willing to make a pledge, but they wanted it to be on terms that reflected their ordering of allegiances. They proposed an alternative wording:

I have pledged my unqualified allegiance and devotion to Jehovah, the Almighty God, and to His Kingdom, for which Jesus commands all Christians to pray.

I respect the flag of the United States and acknowledge it as a symbol of freedom and justice to all.

I pledge allegiance and obedience to all the laws of the United States that are consistent with God's law, as set forth in the Bible.

The West Virginia Board of Education refused this request for a modified pledge and expelled the Witness students. The Witnesses sued again. This time, only three years after it had denied their earlier claims, the Supreme Court overruled its prior decision and sided with the Witnesses.

I think about the Witnesses when I think about past oaths I have taken as a military officer and a lawyer to "support and defend the Constitution of the United States against all enemies, foreign and domestic" and to "bear true faith and allegiance to the same." What if my own faith commitments became "enemies, foreign and domestic," of the Constitution? If that seems implausible, think back to the three-fifths clause and work your way forward. What does it mean to pledge unqualified allegiance to a Constitution that has at various times upheld the enslavement of other human beings, denied the right to vote to women and African Americans, enabled the Japanese-American internment, and facilitated Jim Crow, to name just a few of the more glaring examples? Each of these actions once upheld as constitutional cuts against the core tenets of my faith—and hopefully yours as well.

I no longer swear oaths. I don't even pledge allegiance to the flag or put my hand over my heart during the national anthem. I still stand at attention—as a veteran, I think it's important to honor the significance of these solemn occasions. I just don't want to give them *too much* significance. This has led to occasional awkward moments, like the time I was invited to speak to the Veterans of Foreign Wars and found myself not pledging allegiance from the head table before I began my address to a room full of veterans.

I have also learned over the years that people have strong views about patriotism and the flag. Maybe you do too. Having intense emotion around these ideas and symbols is neither abnormal nor surprising—as the Supreme Court's decision finally vindicating the Jehovah's Witnesses acknowledged:

> The use of an emblem or flag to symbolize some system, idea, institution, or personality is a short-cut from mind to mind. Causes and nations, political parties, lodges, and ecclesiastical groups seek to knit the loyalty of their followings to a flag or banner, a color or design. . . . Associated with many of these symbols are appropriate gestures of acceptance or respect: a salute, a bowed or bared head, a bended knee. A person gets from a symbol the meaning he puts into it, and what is one man's comfort and inspiration is another's jest and scorn.

The challenge for each of us is to leave room for others to render the respect or dissent they deem appropriate without insisting that our loyalties become theirs. That's especially difficult when it comes to patriotism that unfolds against the backdrop of generations of sacrifice. But we can also acknowledge that not everyone has experienced this country the same way, and some people have suffered at its hands rather than on its behalf.

Once you recognize that some of your friends and neighbors lack the intensity or even the directionality of your own loyalties, you can aspire toward a kind of patriotic unity that does not depend on uniformity. As with other faith commitments, you will likely find that encouraging greater honesty about differing beliefs leads to more authentic relationships.

These feelings of patriotism vary across different communities and different regions of the country. Our law school is not too caught up in them. But we have our own kind of religious faith, complete with creeds, liturgies, and heresies. And, as with many of our peer institutions, January brings our one high holy day—Martin Luther King Jr. Day.

I am glad we have MLK Day on the calendar, and I would much rather commemorate the contributions of Dr. King than someone like Christopher Columbus. What intrigues me about the holiday is its singular role in the school's liturgies. Our communications team sends out MLK quotes over social media. We have MLK Day dinners, T-shirts, and buttons. We have speakers, reflections, and pronouncements. Some years, we have even managed to transform MLK Day into MLK Week, with even more speakers, reflections, and pronouncements.

I am also fascinated—and a little put off—by the various efforts to remake Dr. King in our own image. The law school studiously avoids any mention of his Christian faith. Meanwhile, the white people at church always pick the most Jesus-sounding quote they can find from King. Neither really hits the mark. King was complex. He was deeply Christian, though not without his demons. And he probably was not "the right kind of Christian" for someone like Jack Cunningham, my occasional golfing buddy from church.

I bring up my thoughts about MLK Day with Gary on our walk after the January faculty meeting. It's freezing outside. I'm wearing a winter coat, gloves, and a scarf, and I'm still cold.

Gary likes the MLK Day rituals, and he is not buying my critique. "People here seem just fine with vague inspirations like 'justice' and 'equality.' Isn't that enough?"

I am reminded of our conversation last fall after the 9/11 protest and the difference between fairness as following procedures and fairness as adhering to what is good and right. The MLK Day rituals bug me because they fall somewhere in the middle. The glowing platitudes that emerge over the course of these commemorations gesture toward something more than procedural fairness. But these gestures seem largely detached from the rest of the year, much like I imagine Christmas celebrations feel to non-Christians who like the food but don't care for the underlying message or its implications.

Gary isn't wrong about this half-baked arrangement working for people. I'm just not sure how it all holds together over time. Can we really inspire the next generation with vague words and one high holy day?

We learn the news about Stacy Terrill two days after MLK Day. The dean had been notified only a few hours before, after the police had contacted Stacy's parents in Ohio. Stacy was a third-year student living off campus, and she had taken her own life in her apartment. We don't hear many details from the dean, and we won't learn much in the coming weeks, other than some general references to mental health concerns.

I knew Stacy vaguely. She had been one of the eighty students in my Criminal Law class two years earlier. She made smart comments and seemed well-liked by her peers. She was going to make a great lawyer.

I reach out to a few students who were close to Stacy during our Criminal Law class to see how they're doing. They are devastated. There will be a memorial service in a few days at the Lutheran church just off the campus.

Over the years, I have occasionally encountered students who shift noticeably from active and engaged to distant and withdrawn. Sometimes I am aware of the reasons because they tell me; other times I am left speculating. When this shift happens to students I am currently teaching, I can observe it in real time and initiate a conversation based on what I'm seeing in the classroom. I had not seen Stacy since Criminal Law, other than a few passing hellos. She always seemed fine to me, as much as you can tell from a hallway greeting. But obviously she wasn't fine.

The service a few days later is lovely and awful. As I listen to the pastor speak, I realize that part of the awfulness is recognizing there won't be any answers. I spend much of my life searching for answers to problems, either my own or someone else's. And in most cases, I rely on my expertise or judgment to find those answers. I don't like to admit it, but it gives me a sense of control. But when there are no answers, there is no control.

Without answers or control, we are left with either faith or despair. Most of us choose faith, and we place that faith in something—in God, in science, in other people, in ourselves. Most of us live between certain absolutes and absolute uncertainty. We do not prove our beliefs like mathematical equations or lab experiments, but we affirm our commitments to them in the way we live our lives. When we recognize that everyone places their trust in some kind of faith, we can more easily relate to those around us. Even though our actual beliefs and commitments may differ, the uncertainty and vulnerability that come from acting in faith can remind all of us of our shared human condition.

Can Anything Be Neutral?

You can't be neutral on
a moving train.

Howard Zinn

February

is the time of the year I start wistfully hoping for spring, knowing I still have a few months of disappointment ahead of me. At this point in the semester, we are getting into the weeds of free exercise analysis in my Law and Religion class. Like most areas of law, the analysis is more complicated than the headlines suggest. Free exercise cases involve a clash between an asserted right to engage in a religious belief or practice and an asserted government interest restricting that right. Today's class examines various kinds of government interests, which brings us to a case about snake handling in the Appalachian Mountains of Tennessee.

Swann v. Pack is the Law and Religion version of the "cannibalism on the high seas" case that I cover in Criminal Law. I'm not teaching it so my students can more ably represent snake handlers. But the underlying tensions nicely illustrate how our judgments about the limits on religious practice are seldom if ever "neutral." And the facts are memorable.

Liston Pack is pastor of the Holiness Church of God in Jesus Name in Newport, Tennessee. The church derives some of its beliefs and practices from chapter 16 in the gospel of Mark, specifically verses 17 and 18, which in the King James Version read as follows:

And these signs shall follow them that believe; In my name
shall they cast out devils; they shall speak with new tongues;
they shall take up serpents; and if they drink any deadly
thing, it shall not hurt them; they shall lay hands on the sick,
and they shall recover.

Pack and other church leaders are criminally charged for
handling snakes and drinking strychnine at a church service in
April 1973. Two church members drank strychnine and died;
Pack handled the snakes. The case gained some notoriety and
the local prosecutor became concerned that the region was
"in imminent danger and likely to become the snake handling
capital of the world."

The Tennessee courts made a mess of this case. The trial
court said snake handling was not okay but drinking strychnine
was fine, which made no sense. The first appellate court said
snakes were fine as long as everyone consented. The second
appellate court, which issued the opinion I assign to my
students, said no snakes and no strychnine.

The interesting question is why no snakes. I turn to
Susanna Clark, a quiet third-year student from Houston who
usually sits toward the back of the room.

"Susanna, what is the government's interest in preventing
people from handling poisonous snakes in religious
ceremonies?"

I tell Susanna to assume that everyone is a willing
participant and no kids are present. This is one of the best
parts of law school. I can frame a hypothetical to force students
to grapple with the precise issue I want them to confront.

"But what about the person who doesn't realize there are going to be snakes?" asks Susanna.

"I told you everyone consented; don't fight the hypo."

"Fighting the hypo" is a common response by law students to hard questions from professors. It comes up most often when students sense the logical conclusion of their reasoning is fundamentally wrong. It's my job to box them into the hypo to force them to confront the tension between their intuitions and where those intuitions lead them.

Susanna continues, "What about harm to children?"

"There aren't any kids in this hypo."

"But the court's opinion mentioned kids might have been present."

"Yes, but not in my hypo."

Susanna pauses for a bit. "Well, if the state can't restrict consensual snake handling, can it restrict consensual human sacrifice?"

I am delighted to hear the question. I have been telling my students since the semester began that there is no such thing as an absolute right, and if they are ever in doubt, just think about human sacrifice. This advice is generalizable. If you find yourself in an argument brushing up against a seemingly absolutist claim, try to think of an absurd example that disproves the absolute. If you find yourself talking with someone who says they tolerate everyone, ask them about the Nazis. If your interlocutor insists that everyone should be able to pursue their own morality, ask them about child abusers.

In the midst of our discussion about consensual snake handling, Susanna remembers my advice and raises the example of human sacrifice.

"Yes," I respond, "of course the state can restrict human sacrifice."

Even if it's consensual. Though, honestly, I would have my doubts about consent under those circumstances. But let's assume consensual human sacrifice; it's a hypo, after all.

What's the difference between human sacrifice and snake handling? Well, for one thing, intent. The person agreeing to be the object of human sacrifice intends to die—that's kind of the point. The person handling the snakes does not intend to die. In fact, the snake handler is certain they will not die. And they are usually right. By the time this case rolled around, Liston Pack had handled dozens of snakes, and thus far he had a perfect record of not dying.

This brings us to another meaningful difference between human sacrifice and snake handling. The chance of death with human sacrifice is 100 percent. The chance of death with snake handling is significantly lower. It's hard to quantify with any precision, but it just doesn't happen that much.

You know what else has a low but nonzero risk of death? Football. And also parachuting, bungee jumping, and running ultramarathons. The prosecutor in the Tennessee mountains isn't trying to ban any of *those* activities. People risk their lives with all kinds of recreational activities for all kinds of reasons that are arguably less important than "God told me I had to do it." So what's the deal with snake handling? That we don't like it? That it's weird? That it doesn't feel *civilized*? When we think hard about it, there's no nonneutral way to limit the religious freedom of Liston Pack and his merry band of followers. It's a value-based judgment all the way down.

These questions about the elusiveness of neutrality become even harder when we turn to educating kids, which is the subject of our next few classes in Law and Religion. Kids are not just blank slates confronting a bunch of neutral influences. Every decision, every influence, every conversation, nudges them in one direction or another. And plenty of people are actively trying to shape what those kids believe. Parents, teachers, advertisers, musicians, social media stars—we are all clamoring for influence. And parents with deeply held values, which turns out to be most of us, would just as well prefer that our kids share our values. Even supposedly open-minded parents usually want their kids to adopt the value of open-mindedness.

I knew some of this before I had kids of my own, but there is a lot I did not know—and could not have known without being a parent. I could not have known what it feels like to risk having my kids influenced by all the people who are not me. I could not have known what it means to love my kids even when their choices reflect those other influences more than mine. I share some of these thoughts with my students before jumping into today's cases. A few parents in the class nod along, but most of my students do not yet have children of their own.

Our principal case today is *Wisconsin v. Yoder*. The Amish want an exemption from compulsory attendance laws so they can teach their high-school-aged kids the Amish way of life instead of whatever kids learn in non-Amish school. The

Amish are fine if their kids attend public school in their early years, since, as the Supreme Court reminds us, it's good for everyone to know the "three R's." The three R's, of course, are reading, 'riting, and 'rithmetic. Apparently, nineteenth-century educators and twentieth-century Supreme Court justices thought this was a good phonetic device to remember the core elements of a proper education.

The Court decides that the Amish can homeschool their high-school-aged kids. But the analysis is a bit over the top, suggesting that the real reason the Amish win the case is because they are Amish. Here is an actual sentence from Chief Justice Burger's opinion: "The Amish communities singularly parallel and reflect many of the virtues of Jefferson's ideal of the 'sturdy yeoman' who would form the basis of what he considered as the ideal of a democratic society"—as if somehow these "sturdy yeomen" are more deserving of constitutional rights than the rest of us. And then Burger doubles down: "Even their idiosyncratic separateness exemplifies the diversity we profess to admire and encourage."

I am all for protecting the Amish, but it's not because they are Amish and it's not because I admire their idiosyncratic separateness. It's because I believe private groups in civil society should for the most part be able to do what they want, even when what they want to do is at odds with mainstream norms.

None of these positions are neutral. Deciding that private groups should have autonomy or face regulation is a nonneutral, value-laden decision. Protecting the ways of the Amish and denying protections to the snake handlers in the Holiness Church of God in Jesus Name in Newport,

Tennessee, are nonneutral decisions. When it comes to clashes that emerge at the intersection of law and religion, there are no neutral answers.

Our next class session tackles religious influence in public school curricula. To tee up this discussion, I assign a somewhat dated but smartly written article titled "How Christian Were the Founders?" The article chronicles the textbook selection battles in Texas. The state of Texas orders so many public school textbooks—forty-eight million annually—that it effectively sets the market for the rest of the country. You might think that California would play a role, but as the article's author wryly notes, "California is the largest textbook market, but besides being bankrupt, it tends to be so specific about what kinds of information its students should learn that few other states follow its lead." That puts Texas in the driver's seat.

The importance of the textbook market in Texas means textbook selection decisions are really important, which means the Texas State Board of Education is really important. And the conservative Christians have figured this out. The article I assign details some of the characters and personalities who make their way into the decision-making process. It's a pretty wild story, including a dentist named Don whose "real passions are his faith and the state board of education." Don is a "young earth" creationist who thinks "textbooks are mostly the product of the liberal establishment."

The Texans in my class tell me all of this is entirely plausible, and they recall their public school textbooks having some weird stories in them. They seem no worse for wear, college having disabused them of these fanciful historical takes. Better still, college has taught them to be *open-minded*, unlike Don the dentist. I ask them if they're open-minded enough to be okay if their kids grow up to be like Don.

This exchange transitions to a robust discussion about whether any classroom or textbook can really be neutral. One of my students notes astutely that even the best math teachers make nonneutral decisions about content and pedagogy; for example, the decision whether to teach linear algebra rather than advanced calculus can nudge students toward different career possibilities. And that's to say nothing of racial, gender, and other biases held by teachers across a variety of disciplines.

I think about this all the time in my own teaching. I try to minimize my biases and encourage rich discussion about the topics at hand. But I also self-consciously set nonneutral limits on the scope of acceptable arguments. When I teach Law and Religion, I don't take seriously suggestions that the United States should be a theocracy, nor do I entertain arguments that the government should shut down churches. Those political arrangements might be plausible in other countries, but they are not relevant to the legal and cultural realities that frame my teaching at an American law school. We can use the extremes as thought experiments but not as serious arguments.

Having said that, recognizing the lack of neutrality in

textbooks and classrooms does not mean we surrender the search for truth. We can all acknowledge truth in the world and at times be confident we have found it. We all believe in the mechanics that make cars and airplanes work, the distinctions that tell us some plants are poisonous and others are not, and the theory of gravity. It would be next to impossible to live otherwise.

We also all believe in moral truths. Almost all of us believe the Holocaust was evil and the end of slavery was good. In asserting these beliefs—and many others—we set limits on the scope of the debates we are willing to have. Those nonneutral limits are all around us, and they are crucial to fending off an open-ended relativism.

The question for classrooms—and also for governments and societies—is not whether we achieve neutrality but whether we pursue knowledge and wisdom while interrogating reigning orthodoxies and allowing for reasonable dissent. When it comes to education and politics, almost everything hinges on what is "reasonable," not on what is "objective." That in turn rests more on persuasion than pronouncement.

Once we recognize the importance of persuasion, we can move toward engaging people in conversations instead of merely asserting conclusions. This is increasingly important at a time when authority and expertise face mounting skepticism and when countless pundits tell us they are "fair and balanced" or are "the most trusted name in news." The fair and balanced truth is that there is no way to cover the news neutrally because the news usually involves a great deal of nonneutral complexity.

So too with the law. Judges even divide the way they

think about cases into "questions of fact" and "questions of law." Some questions of fact are disputed, but they are ultimately answered conclusively—the contract expired last Tuesday, the defendant stole the money, the company paid its debt. Judges also decide questions of law, but these are not neutral decisions. They are judgments about how best to understand facts of the world in light of relevant legal frameworks.

You and I do something similar in our ordinary lives. For example, my daughter Lauren and I both know that she dented my new car forty-eight hours after getting her license (a fact of the world), but we probably disagree about the aesthetics of the dent or whether repairing it is worth the cost (judgments related to what should happen). And this is a relatively benign example. We exercise far weightier nonneutral judgments throughout our lives. Rather than simply insisting we are right, we might embrace the challenge of looking for the values underlying our assumptions and work to persuade others with our words and acts. (Of course, as Lauren can tell you, some efforts at persuasion are more successful than others.)

The Sunday after my classroom discussion about the Texas State Board of Education, I am on my way to grab a second doughnut in the fellowship hall at church when I spot Jack Cunningham standing by himself a few feet away from the snack table. I snag a doughnut and head in his direction.

Jack perks up when he sees me approaching. "Hey,

Professor, did you see yesterday's *Wall Street Journal* article about a liberal school board in Massachusetts pushing to teach revisionist history?"

I can never tell whether Jack intends "Professor" as an honorific or a subtle insult, but today I assume good intentions. After catching up a bit about our families, he summarizes the article while I attend to 700 calories' worth of sprinkle-covered chocolate goodness.

Jack is not happy about the proposed curricular changes in Massachusetts.

"Well, what do you think they should be teaching?" I ask him.

"The true story of America. That America was founded as a Christian nation."

I think he's baiting me, but I'm not sure. "Well, suppose you are on the school board and you are arguing that a high school history class should teach America's Christian founding. But suppose another member of the board—let's call her Kate—thinks the truth is that this country was founded on racism and slavery. And let's say you both really believe in your convictions. What happens then?"

We go back and forth for about ten minutes. In the midst of our discussion, I think of how the tension between Jack and my hypothetical school board member Kate derives more from their deeply held beliefs than from observable facts. Neither Jack nor Kate can really prove their truth.

At this point I'm invested in this conversation, but I spot Hana and Sam bickering in the corner. So I tell Jack we'll pick up the discussion sometime on the golf course, and I walk over to enforce the peace between my kids. But I am still

mulling over my conversation with Jack later that afternoon.
In my hypothetical, Jack and Kate are unable to translate
their beliefs—they cannot get into each other's heads enough
to fully understand why the other person could possibly hold
such beliefs. They both think they have the morally correct
way of educating children. And neither can demonstrate their
viewpoints like a mathematical proof. They are both just sure
of their views, and they both want to impose those views on
other people's children.

The stakes feel enormous, especially when we move
beyond the questions about the Texas State Board of Education
to state legislatures defining criminal offenses, boardrooms
of big tech companies deciding censorship norms, and lots of
other political, economic, and social institutions that shape
how we live our lives and form our values—all in deeply
nonneutral ways.

The next day, I discover Jennifer Chang's thesis draft waiting
in my inbox. My initial curiosity turns to frustration. She
clearly has taken none of my suggestions, opting instead to
double down on some of her more strident assertions. But the
most disappointing part of reading her draft is seeing flashes
of brilliance scattered throughout her myopic arguments.
Sometimes I read an unsatisfying student draft and think, *She
needs to work harder*. With Jennifer, I think to myself, *She is
unteachable*.

I decide to wait a day before sending my feedback to
Jennifer. I always find it challenging to respond with the right

mix of candor and encouragement, but I find it particularly difficult with Jennifer's draft:

- You need to work on the precision of your claims, and you will be best served by sticking closely to the text of the claims you want to critique.
- You write that Augustine "always" makes this assumption, but this is factually inaccurate.
- I don't see how your objection challenges the claim you quote.
- You would be more persuasive if you argue that this interpretation of Augustine is "misguided" rather than "preposterous." The author you are critiquing is a leading scholar in the field and has spent a lot of time developing this argument. You don't have to agree with him, but you should take him seriously.
- Your normative beliefs are not neutral views that everyone assumes to be true.

Jennifer will have the rest of the semester to complete her independent study. I have no doubt that it will be well-written and meticulously cited. But it is shaping up to be a diatribe rather than a work of persuasion. This is the challenge of making normative arguments. Once you have realized how much of the world is not neutral—how much of it is up for grabs—it's natural to want to argue for your view of how things should be. Few of us want to live in a world determined more by the arguments we detest than the arguments we embrace. But persuading others that you have the better account begins by recognizing the biases and judgments implicit in your own views and addressing the best possible counterarguments with charity and clarity. More often than not, if you start with this posture, you will be able to engage with others more effectively and less stridently. Recognizing a lack of neutrality does not mean embracing a lack of nuance.

Where Is the **Line between Wrong and Evil?**

Each of us is more than the worst thing we've ever done.

Bryan Stevenson

In March, my Law and Religion class turns to three Supreme Court cases involving the Mormons, known today as the Church of Jesus Christ of Latter-day Saints. Early in their history, the Mormons were polygamists, or, more precisely, the church required male members with the financial means to support more than one wife to be polygamists. It was also the time of westward expansion, and the Mormons kept getting kicked out of towns by intolerant Protestants, some of whom assaulted and murdered them along the way. After fleeing a series of these persecutions, the Mormons eventually settled near the Great Salt Lake, which was federal territory at the time.

Whether the federal government could restrict polygamy in the territories got tied up in whether the federal government could restrict slavery in the territories, so the people wanting to restrict polygamy waited until the South seceded to ensure they had the votes. By that time, the federal troops were too busy fighting a war to enforce territorial laws, so the Mormons got a pass for a few years.

The hammer dropped after Appomattox. It included the federal prosecution of George Reynolds, the secretary to church president Brigham Young. The feds prosecuted him under something called the Morrill Act, which prohibited a person who was already married from marrying someone else.

I begin by asking the class why George Reynolds felt compelled to disobey the law. "What was at stake for him?" At this point in the semester, I have usually moved away from any cold calling, especially in an upper-level class. So my question hangs in the air for a few seconds while a few students decide whether they want to weigh in.

Scott Thompson eventually raises a hand. "According to the Supreme Court's opinion, the penalty for choosing otherwise under church doctrine would be damnation in the life to come."

That's important. Polygamy isn't just a merit badge for George Reynolds; it's a prerequisite for his salvation.

"And, Scott, what does the Court say in response to that claim?"

"The First Amendment protects beliefs but not actions."

"Right." It gets more complicated a few decades later, but this is basically the nineteenth-century standard. "And what's their authority for this distinction between beliefs and actions?"

"Thomas Jefferson."

A good rule of thumb is that when the Court turns to Jefferson in a religion case, the decision will have a fairly narrow view of religious liberty. James Madison, in contrast, usually signals a broader view. I am not sure this holds in all cases, but it works most of the time. And it works in this case.

The Court seems especially concerned with polygamy. I ask Scott to flip to the third page of the opinion and give us the Court's reasoning. He begins reading:

> Suppose one believed that human sacrifices were a
> necessary part of religious worship, would it be seriously

contended that the civil government under which he lived could not interfere to prevent a sacrifice? Or if a wife religiously believed it was her duty to burn herself upon the funeral pile of her dead husband, would it be beyond the power of the civil government to prevent her carrying her belief into practice?

See! The Court is also using human sacrifice as a limit case. But something more nefarious is going on in this part of the Court's opinion. It's an old trick: mention A and B that are *very bad* and then imply that C is also *very bad*. It's not the tightest legal reasoning, but it's often effective. In this case, the Court is suggesting that the Mormons are not just *wrong* for practicing polygamy; they're *evil*.

Scott jumps back in to suggest that there is a lot of daylight between human sacrifice and polygamy. He is certainly right from our modern vantage point, but this was less clear to the people living at the end of the nineteenth century.

George Reynolds lost his case at the Supreme Court and went to prison. A few years later, Congress passed a similar law aimed at the Idaho territory, this one requiring a person to swear that they are not a member of any organization that teaches or encourages polygamy and that they will not teach, advise, counsel, or encourage any person to commit the "crime of bigamy or polygamy."

I open the discussion of the second case with a comparative question: "What's the difference between the Idaho law and the earlier law that ensnared Reynolds?" At this point, I'm all in on Scott. He has clearly read these cases carefully and is interested in the conversation.

Scott pauses for just a moment and then suggests, "It's one thing to say you can't *practice* polygamy. But now Congress is saying you can't *teach* polygamy."

"Yes, and in fact, this law goes beyond even a prohibition on teaching. You can't even belong to a group that teaches or encourages polygamy."

You could be unmarried with no prospect for a wife, let alone more than one. You could disagree with the doctrine. None of that matters. Membership alone makes you culpable. And the feds get you by making you swear an oath and then accusing you of lying—the playbook for authoritarians from the Salem witch trials to the loyalty hearings of McCarthyism and the Red Scare.

There is one more Supreme Court case, and this time the feds aren't fooling around. They yank the charter from the Mormon Church, dissolve their legal status, and seize their assets. It is the single greatest act of religious persecution in the history of the United States—the federal government using the force of law to destroy an entire religion.

Shortly after this last case, the church changed their doctrine, President William Henry Harrison granted them amnesty, and they got back their property. Utah obtained statehood a few years later, with a proviso banning polygamy. But this wasn't compromise; it was forced surrender. And it was premised on the view that polygamy could not be tolerated. You can tolerate wrong; you can't tolerate evil.

What happens when our understanding of evil changes over time? In 2022, three out of four Americans responding to a Gallup poll indicated they believed polygamy was "morally wrong." But that no longer translates to a view that it should be legally prohibited. Since the Supreme Court constitutionalized gay marriage in 2015, most anti-polygamy laws have either fallen off the books or been refashioned into less substantial violations. The line that seems to be emerging is that you can marry whomever you want absent abusive or fraudulent circumstances, as long as everyone is of the specified age. Utah recently changed its law criminalizing bigamy from a felony to an infraction. So getting a second wife in Utah these days is about as consequential as driving forty-five in a thirty-five-mph speed zone. Which might be another way of saying that even if most people in Utah still think polygamy is wrong, they no longer think it is evil.

If people can see polygamy as wrong without deeming it evil, then what about support for or opposition to gay marriage? Is either support for gay marriage or opposition to it evil? We get to these questions a few days later in *Masterpiece Cakeshop v. Colorado Civil Rights Commission*. This is the case about the guy who does not want to bake a cake for a gay couple's wedding.

This case frustrates me for two reasons. The first is that I have rarely encountered public commentary that musters an ounce of empathy for the other side. People who think the guy should bake the cake can't fathom that his religious objection might actually be sincere. And people who think the guy should not have to bake the cake can't see that the gay couple might actually have experienced emotional harm from the denial. I am generalizing a bit, but if you look back at the media coverage as the case was being litigated, it is hard to find much nuance.

The second reason that *Masterpiece Cakeshop* frustrates

me is that the Supreme Court tells us almost nothing useful. Instead of a constitutional analysis, Justice Kennedy gives us a great deal of . . . Justice Kennedy's views: *Gay people are nice. Religious people are nice. The Colorado officials who first decided this case were not nice. Everyone should be nice to each other and respect each other's dignity.*

I am not kidding—go read the opinion if you don't believe me. And it's not that I don't want people to be nice to each other. But "Be nice" doesn't usually translate into constitutional doctrine. And in place of guidelines for lower courts and policymakers, we get some Justice Kennedy-isms. Here's one:

> When it comes to weddings, it can be assumed that a member of the clergy who objects to gay marriage on moral and religious grounds could not be compelled to perform the ceremony without denial of his or her right to the free exercise of religion. This refusal would be well understood in our constitutional order as an exercise of religion, an exercise that gay persons could recognize and accept without serious diminishment to their own dignity and worth.

I certainly don't think clergy should be compelled to perform wedding ceremonies. But I don't see why gay people would just "recognize and accept" that assertion "without serious diminishment to their own dignity and worth." I would think some gay people would be fine if some clergy don't want to marry them, and others would be deeply offended. It's not hard to imagine a scenario where a gay couple asks a pastor to marry them only to find out the pastor doesn't officiate gay weddings and thereafter suffers emotional harm from this news and rejection. If clergy are constitutionally different from cake bakers, it can't be "because Justice Kennedy says so."

Here is another Justice Kennedy-ism from the decision:

> If that exception [for clergy] were not confined, then a long list of persons who provide goods and services for marriages and weddings might refuse to do so for gay persons, thus resulting in a community-wide stigma inconsistent with the history and dynamics of civil rights laws that ensure equal access to goods, services, and public accommodations.

Well, I don't want gay people facing "community-wide stigma." But it's not clear to me how a guy refusing to bake a cake in Denver could lead to that result. It turns out that in *Masterpiece Cakeshop*, the gay couple found a bakery down the street that would bake their cake for free. And while Denver isn't Berkeley or San Francisco, it is progressive enough that a gay couple facing a wall of exclusion for their wedding seems highly unlikely.

I wish Justice Kennedy had paid more attention to contextual differences and situations where the possibility of community-wide stigma is not a hypothetical. Take a small rural town in the South with one bakery. The gay couple denied a wedding cake in that town might well have no other options. And in that small town, it's possible that the florist and the local bed-and-breakfast might also object to the wedding. All of that starts to feel a lot like "community-wide stigma" that prevents the couple from "equal access to goods, services, and public accommodations."

What do we do in *that* situation? The religious beliefs of

the rural baker may be just as sincere as those of the Denver baker, but the surrounding context is quite different. The strongest proponents of religious freedom would say the differences in my small-town hypothetical shouldn't matter and the religious claimant should always prevail.

I ask my students what they think, and the question leads to a discussion about various rights and harms.

Kirk Rhodes, a third-year student from Atlanta, suggests that sometimes religious freedom claims should lose to antidiscrimination laws.

Olivia Kingston, a second year from St. Paul, isn't sure where to draw the line. She notes that the First Amendment singles out religion for special protection, which might make a religious baker different from a nonreligious baker.

"But what about all of the people arguing that the baker's cake is art?" asks Kirk. "If art is speech and artistic speech always wins, then couldn't anyone refuse to bake a cake for anyone else? How do we draw a line?"

Olivia pushes back on Kirk: "That's a hard question, but it's not the question the Court decided in this case. This case was about the free exercise of religion."

Our discussion is far better than what I remember of the media coverage and dueling op-eds surrounding the case when Justice Kennedy sided with the cake baker. Or, for that matter, the public commentary surrounding a host of other legal clashes between progressives and religious conservatives over gay marriage and related issues. There was the case about the Catholic adoption agency in Philadelphia that did not want to place kids with same-sex couples. Then there was the website designer who did not want to make a website for gay weddings.

And along the way, the 2022 Respect for Marriage Act recognized gay marriage at the federal level and acknowledged that religious freedom means that people can hold different views about the morality of gay marriage.

In some ways, the Respect for Marriage Act represents the kind of political compromise that works even though neither extreme really likes it. On the one hand, it codifies legal protection for same-sex marriage (which most people support) and interracial marriage (which almost everyone supports). On the other hand, it recognizes that "reasonable and sincere people" hold diverse beliefs about marriage based on "decent and honorable religious or philosophical premises."

The extreme conservatives don't like this law because they want a country that bans same-sex marriage. The extreme progressives don't like the law because they want a country where everyone whose religious beliefs don't support same-sex marriage is deemed a hateful bigot. The Respect for Marriage Act pushes back on both extremes and says that neither being in a same-sex marriage nor expressing religious opposition to same-sex marriage is evil. It suggests that when it comes to this issue, we can still live in a world where we view each other as wrong—even deeply wrong—without crossing the line to evil.

I suppose this looks a lot like Justice Kennedy's *Masterpiece Cakeshop* opinion after all. But the source of authority matters. A one-judge philosophy of who counts as "nice" isn't going to hold this country together. Bipartisan legislation reinforced with coalitions built across the aisle has a chance of rooting policy interests in the lives of actual human beings, most of whom don't view each other as fundamentally evil but who could use a few reminders of why that is the case.

In Wednesday's Law and Religion class, we are tackling a different set of issues and diving into the subtleties of ceremonial prayer and religious monuments. One of the key questions is whether longstanding historical practices are somehow constitutionally different than more recent practices. But the line drawing gets complicated. If a ceremonial prayer before the legislature is not okay, then what about a prayer before a state funeral? If it's okay to have "In God We Trust" on our money, then why can't that also be the official motto of a state or town? If St. Louis and Corpus Christi don't need to change their names, then could a new town name itself "Jesus Town"?

We are a few minutes into discussing these questions when we hear an emergency alert. Anyone who has been a student or teacher in the last twenty years knows about these alerts. Something bad has happened, has possibly happened, or might happen. Everybody needs to know about it and take immediate action.

The motivation behind emergency alerts is good; the execution is not. All at once, every cell phone in the class starts buzzing with automated texts and voice messages. Students with open computers start getting emergency emails with lots of capital letters and exclamation points. A loud siren wails in the background, followed by some automated voice muttering unintelligible words in an ominous tone.

The first step is to determine whether the alert signals severe weather, an active shooter, or an unscheduled system test. The initial buzzes and sirens unhelpfully sound exactly the same for all of these situations. Today, the alert warns of an active shooter, which understandably sets off anxieties. We hear the magnetic locks click shut and dutifully move a few desks to block the doors. Then we sit together in silence for a few minutes. We don't hear anything—no other sirens, no emergency vehicles, no SWAT teams. We are all just waiting, a bit unnerved. In thirty minutes, we will get the all-clear and return to normal. But not yet. For now, we are locked in this classroom with nowhere to go and everyone's anxiety rising.

Nobody seems in the mood to get back to our discussion of ceremonial prayer. So to fill the time, and because it's generally on theme with the alert, I tell them about my experience as a young lawyer at the Pentagon on 9/11. I was in my office trying to broker a mediation with the Maryland attorney general's office. My paralegal peeked in to tell me that a plane had hit the Twin Towers in New York. I thought to myself, *What a terrible accident!* Then I went back to more calls with the Maryland lawyers. My paralegal returned to report that some people were saying it might not be an accident. We walked together to my boss's office to watch the news and arrived just in time to see the second plane hit. Clearly not an accident. Back at my desk, I called my mom to tell her what was going on and ask her to say a prayer. Then I was back on the phone with the Maryland lawyers. Then I heard the plane coming in, very low and very loud.

The plane hit the other side of the building, and I did not even hear the impact. Just a long period of silence followed by a great deal of commotion.

The next stretch of time is one I have never quite nailed

down in my memory. My boss and I ran out of our office and into the D-Ring corridor. We were never in immediate danger, but we did not know that at the time as we tried a few different ways to exit the building through smoke and screams. And then we were out under the clear blue sky, watching an enormous cloud of smoke billowing up from the other side of the building and trying to reach coworkers and family members on overloaded phone systems that could not handle the call volume.

We were back to work the next morning, trying to ignore the smoke that seemed to be everywhere. The building was still on fire, and the emergency crews were still conducting search and rescue a few hundred feet away. Donald Rumsfeld, the Secretary of Defense, had declared to the world that the Pentagon was open for business, and he had ordered us back to work to prove it. I imagine most of the people in the building the day after 9/11 were directing special forces and combat air patrols. But at least one of us was sitting in a smoke-filled office brokering a mediation with the Maryland attorney general's office.

The Pentagon story is a good reminder of evil in the world. Our Law and Religion class has spent the past few months tackling some of the most contentious cultural clashes. My students often have strong opinions coming into class, and part of my job as a teacher is to get them to see that well-intentioned people can have differing beliefs without being evil. Let's save the "evil" label for the active shooters and the people who fly planes into buildings.

A few days later, I am working in my office when I hear a knock at my door and look up to see Joseph Villario, the Navy veteran I met during orientation who ended up in my Criminal Law class last semester. I realize I have not seen Joe since the exam review session last semester.

"Sir, may I come in?"

"Sure thing, Joe. What's on your mind?"

"Is it okay if I shut the door?"

Joe begins by telling me he did not expect law school to be this hard. Despite working long hours and studying diligently for exams, he did poorly in his first-semester classes, and now he is worried about the coming spring exams. Fifteen minutes later, Joe is fighting back tears. He knew there would be pressure, but he hadn't worried too much because it wasn't the kind of life-and-death pressure he had faced in the military. And what will the Navy think of one of its officers breaking down in his professor's office over the pressures of law school? I reassure Joe that the Navy will not hear about this conversation. And I tell him that, yes, this stuff matters, but it's not the most important thing in the world. And being in The Middle—or, as it turns out, in Joe's case, The Bottom—is not easy. But things are going to be okay. I have no doubt that Joe is going to make a great lawyer, and I tell him as much.

The more we talk, the more I realize how discouraged Joe is at being in The Bottom. It's particularly soul-crushing for Joe because it's his first taste of real failure—all-state high school athlete in Arizona, United States Naval Academy, graduate of the Navy's Nuclear Power School, excellent fitness reports in his first two duty stations, and selection for the competitive legal education program that brought him here. And now—The Bottom.

To be honest, I am a little surprised that Joe is having this much difficulty. After all, he came into law school with a fair amount of life experience. When I met him at orientation, my first thought was that he'd do just fine. But experience isn't everything, and when it comes to what it takes to succeed in law school, there are more exceptions than there are rules. It's another good reminder for me to pay attention to students as individuals and not assume categories like "veteran" mean the same thing for everyone.

Joe's situation is also complicated by his sense of social isolation. He is a white, conservative, military guy, used to being a leader who voices his opinion. He's also no dummy, and it didn't take him long to recognize that the political context of law school was quite different from the ones he encountered at Annapolis or the Naval Submarine Base in Kings Bay, Georgia. Joe tells me he has heeded my orientation advice not to be a First Amendment hero. But for the past few months, every time he has attempted to voice an unorthodox opinion, he has felt shouted down by some of his more vocal classmates. One time during a lunch conversation, Joe said he agreed with the city cops who had ended a local Black Lives Matter protest. The student next to him had told him to shut up and that Joe's white supremacist views were not welcome here.

Things had gotten worse a few weeks ago when Joe mentioned in the class-wide group chat—*why do they have those?*—that he had voted for the Republican candidate based on foreign policy. Given the responses in the group chat, Joe told me, you would have thought he had cast a vote for Hitler. Or that he *was* Hitler.

This is not the first time I have heard this kind of story

from conservative students like Joe. Some of the complaints come across a little too aggrieved, as if this were the kind of thing these students were expecting to find in law school. But Joe's concerns seem different to me. I know him well enough to know he isn't a culture warrior, and the stories he tells me are worrisome. But I am not sure what to say in response, other than to assure Joe that he is going to make a great lawyer and to let him know that my door is always open.

After Joe leaves, I spend the next two hours reflecting on our conversation, unable to finish the manuscript review I had hoped to complete. Wasn't Joe right to be concerned? And isn't there something I can do about it? Don't I bear some responsibility for this institution that is training students to be lawyers?

I am also struck by the question of what counts as an evil opinion. You might think Republicans are a disaster for this country, but large segments of Americans think differently, including a lot of lawyers and future lawyers. And as far as Joe's defense of the protest shutdown, I am in complete agreement with his views. Because my scholarly focus is the First Amendment's right of assembly, I'm usually the one arguing for a robust right to protest. But this particular protest had turned violent when a group of people overturned an empty police car and threw large rocks at the police line. That's not only an unlawful assembly; it's a riot, and the police were well within their discretion to shut it down. It's crazy to me that Joe would be shouted down for making that argument.

In a country as large and diverse as the United States, every one of us holds beliefs and opinions that other people think are beyond the pale. I suppose we could just run around calling each other evil, but that would either heighten tensions or diminish the value of the word. Perhaps it is better to start with the presumption that most people can be wrong—even deeply wrong—without being evil.

One practical way to embrace this presumption is to look for something good about the people you find most wrong. Start with the political leaders you don't like. Try to name one thing they do well, one group of people whose lives they have improved, one way they have contributed to your understanding of human flourishing. Make this a personal effort in the silence of your mind rather than a performative gesture on social media. And if you can't come up with anything, ask yourself if it's because they need to change or because you need to change.

APRIL

Is Forgiveness
Possible?

If we really want to love,
we must learn to forgive.

Mother Teresa

April

is that time of the year when the weather can't make up its mind, but most of us have decided we are ready for spring. The trees are in bloom, the sun is out more often than not, and the air is filled with anticipation. But not everything is as hopeful as the weather.

I hear about the controversy involving the Stanford professor from my research assistant, Kim Riley. She and I are meeting at Whispers—both of us are holding black coffees that are still just a bit too hot to drink. Kim came to law school after running track at Southern Illinois University and graduating with a double major in business and English. I hired her to be one of my research assistants at the end of her first year of law school, and we have worked together closely for the past two years. Kim is focused and competitive, and an incredibly hard worker. Today, sitting across the table with coffee in hand, she is as unsettled as I have ever seen her.

Kim is an editor for our *Law Review*, and she has been working on a Law and Religion symposium they are publishing. One of the symposium authors is a professor at Stanford. The professor, a white man, had been teaching a class on constitutional history at Stanford, talking about the founders' mixed record on liberty, justice, and equality. He noted how some of them had been racist slaveholders even as they espoused that "all men are created equal." To drive home the point, the professor had read a quote attributed to Patrick Henry that contained the n-word. The professor believed reading the full quote was important to demonstrate the ugly context. He warned the class that he was about to read this awful quote and then condemned it after he read it. Some students who weren't in the class learned of the reading of the quote and expressed concerns. The professor met with some of them and told them, upon hearing their concerns, that he would not use the word again.

That wasn't good enough for the students, who started a series of protests against him. It spilled over to our school when some members of our *Law Review* learned of the protests and decided to join in solidarity. They went to the dean and demanded action. They wanted something that would hold the Stanford professor accountable. Kim had stood up against their growing outrage, and she had been excoriated by some of her peers.

Kim can't understand how a professor's classroom decision to convey a word in all of its ugliness is so categorically beyond the pale. She can't understand why his commitment to change his approach after student pushback didn't fully resolve the issue. And she can't understand how her defense of his decision makes her "unsafe" in the eyes of some of her classmates.

The student protesters see it differently. They have witnessed nationwide protests against racial injustice, and they sense a turning point in public opinion about and attention to these matters. They think it is important to show solidarity with others around the country. Their specific course of action is to publish a statement of condemnation of the Stanford professor's article in our *Law Review*.

I am the faculty editor of this symposium, and I have my own interest in protecting its intellectual content. I do not want this protest statement—which has nothing to do with law and religion—inserted into my symposium. And so I meet with the student protesters and with some of my colleagues. We meet for hours and hours, day after day. There is little resolution in sight. During this time, Kim and a few others trickle into my office to express their concerns about the protest. But they are the outliers. Most of the students have convinced themselves that they have a moral duty to protest the Stanford professor. It's not clear to me that the professor violated any clearly established academic norm. I would not have chosen to say the word, but I don't think this is at all a red line that everyone knows is not to be crossed. And if it is, what other red lines are out there, and how do we know?

The students issue their protest statement the following week. They chastise the professor for his "unacceptable" classroom decision and apologize to readers who are hurt by the article they have just published.

I spend the next few days reflecting on what has transpired—the intensity of the student reactions, the escalation to some form of punitive action, and the absence of any grace or nuance in the whole episode. It is discouraging, and a bit frightening. The Stanford professor is a big deal in our faculty circles. If this kind of anger could rage against him, what about the rest of us?

I suppose that tenure protects me against some of these whims. My untenured colleagues who would love to raise difficult issues about justice and injustice in their classes do not have that luxury. And who is to say what the next outrage will be? Is it just the spoken n-word? What if a professor shows a movie clip with the n-word in it instead of reading a quote? What about printed words—can professors even assign Supreme Court opinions that use the word? What if a *student* utters the n-word when responding to a question or reading an opinion—is the professor obliged to rebuke the student for the utterance? Does the new norm extend to other slurs, and why or why not? Every one of these questions is now up for grabs.

On Friday, Gary and I carve out some time to grab lunch at a nearby barbecue joint. We both indulge in a beer, knowing it might dull the afternoon's productivity but feeling like we both deserve it after witnessing our students pillory the Stanford professor. Just after the bill arrives, Gary confides that he is changing the syllabus for his fall class on the Fourteenth Amendment. After seeing what happened to the Stanford professor, he has decided not to cover the recent civil rights protests in our city, opting instead for a comparative look at protests in Hong Kong. The Hong Kong protests are more abstract, more distant. That also makes them less real and less risky. My first thought is about the loss this will be for our students. Gary had participated in some of the local protests, and he could have blended his experience and expertise into a potent teaching moment. But it would have required taking a risk. And after witnessing what happened with the Stanford professor, I don't blame him for not taking that risk.

There is a question deeper than academic freedom that pesters me about this whole incident. The Stanford professor had already committed not to say the word again. So what exactly was the purpose of the ongoing protest directed against him? Did the universe demand some further atonement from him? Did the protesters think it important to "make him an example" as a warning to future would-be transgressors? The latter theory, if right, would be hard to square with a justice-oriented crowd usually wary of scapegoating. This kind of punitive protest—and the lack of grace for the difficulty of navigating these classroom settings—seems bereft of any sense of redemption.

In the middle of April, we turn to the COVID-19 shutdown cases in Law and Religion. When COVID-19 first hit the United States in 2020, it was right around this time of the year. I can still recall the sinking feeling that lingered as everyone tried to calculate the harms and risks of this new virus. The day the law school shut down all outside travel, I was flying back from giving a public lecture. It was during that weird time in the early days of the pandemic when nobody had masks but lots of people were saying you should have masks. And nobody quite knew how the virus spread or how harmful it was. I walked through the airport feeling like I was in the middle of an apocalyptic movie, wondering how many people around me were going to make it. And a few days later, we were stockpiling toilet paper and holding our breath in public restrooms.

State and local governments quickly issued social distancing and shutdown orders. Some of those orders affected churches. And this set up an epic clash of harms at the center of my academic expertise. On the one hand, the orders not only restricted free exercise but also limited what many people consider to be the core of that exercise—religious worship. On the other hand, they did so in order to stop the spread of a deadly virus, a public health interest of the highest order.

The resulting tensions led to dozens of lawsuits, some of which made their way to the Supreme Court. We focus our class discussion on these cases. The pandemic created an oddity for free exercise law. Usually, the free exercise of religion limits officials from granting "secular" exemptions to laws that do not also provide religious exemptions. For example, if a law against killing animals doesn't exempt animal sacrifice in a religious ceremony, it shouldn't exempt hunting either. Under this logic, if churches couldn't open during the pandemic, then nonreligious organizations should also shut down. A law with no exceptions seems really important. A law with nonreligious exceptions is by definition less rigorously enforced, which raises the question of why religious conduct can't be similarly exempted.

The pandemic differed because the response to it required some nonreligious institutions, such as hospitals, to remain open. Because these exceptions to shutdown orders increased the risk of spreading COVID-19, the government's interest in shuttering other institutions—including religious ones— increased. This is because social distancing to prevent the spread of COVID-19 presents a collective action problem; it only works if most people decide to follow along, even if their own individual preferences would have them do otherwise.

If shutdown orders only exempted hospitals and a narrow class of government services, then under certain pandemic conditions, restrictions affecting houses of worship would likely be upheld, even though these restrictions would not be generally applicable. But some states also exempted a dizzying array of other services (including, in some cases, casinos, liquor stores, and bicycle repair shops) that made the orders even less generally applicable. Worse still, some states settled on the unfortunate label "essential activity" to denote businesses and services exempted from generally applicable shutdown orders. The implication was that nonexempted activities were "nonessential."

The strength of the government's public health interest varied considerably during the pandemic. In many cases, it depended on rates of transmission, hospitalization, mortality, and, eventually, vaccination. Given the fast-moving nature of the virus and the lack of coordinated federal guidance, different cases arose under different pandemic conditions. That meant there was no way to generalize the wisdom or constitutionality of a particular ordinance. What was constitutionally defensible in California at a certain stage of the pandemic may or may not have been defensible a few months later in New York. In other words, the specific facts and local conditions of these cases mattered to our understanding of harm. And we were often divided over our interpretations of harm even within the same local context.

I will admit my own pandemic posture at times resembled my approach to driving, where I think everyone moving faster than me is a reckless idiot and everyone moving slower is a lifeless killjoy. One thing is for sure—no one got everything right in the early days of the pandemic. But just a few years later, it seemed like a lot of people were quick to justify their own COVID-19 missteps while demanding repentance from everyone else for theirs.

I wrote about these ideas a while back. I began by

noting that reconciliation—restored relationship between two parties—requires both forgiveness and repentance. And I confessed that I had few ideas for what that kind of reconciliation might look like on a political level in the wake of the pandemic. Perhaps public commentators and public officials should convey forgiveness and repentance to one another and, when appropriate, express repentance to their constituencies. Maybe some of them should face political consequences for their more egregious and harmful policy decisions, including conservative politicians who ignored compelling evidence about COVID-19 mitigation and liberal politicians who ignored compelling evidence about the relatively low risks of in-person schooling.

In my reflections, I suggested to readers that perhaps it was more plausible—and more actionable—to think about forgiveness and repentance in our individual and interpersonal relationships, with friends and family whose pandemic choices have complicated and, in some cases, wounded our relationships.

The responses were swift and . . . unforgiving.

Dave R.: *"No forgiveness. Never. And there will be no quarter."*

Maureen B.: *"Your essay is nothing but self-serving BS. And for what it's worth, speak for yourself. Some of us have no COVID missteps to apologize for. Not all of us have made pandemic mistakes."*

Paul W.: *"F*ck you. You and everyone else who ruined people's lives should get the worst kind of cancer. Eat sh*t and die."* (asterisks mine)

141

These and several hundred other angry responses flowed into my inbox and across my social media feeds. And they came from both directions—some people angry at the suggestion that we should forgive those who fought for protective measures, others unwilling to forgive those who didn't fight hard enough for such measures. The striking unwillingness to forgive may reflect both pain and rage at loss and injustice. But it may also be the case that the very idea of forgiveness has become offensive to many people in our society.

Perhaps you have sensed this in some of your own circles. Our broken relationships feel more irreparable and our interpersonal scorekeeping is harder to let go. The absence of forgiveness is a sobering possibility for you and for me as individuals; its implications for society seem even more dire. But an openness to forgiveness will in some ways require an openness to our own faults and shortcomings. Whatever the truth of the world may be, it's not fully my truth, and it's not fully yours. The more we insist our missteps are justified while demanding that others repent before we can forgive, the more we will harden ourselves, our neighbors, and ultimately our society.

At the end of April, I fly to Los Angeles to speak at a conference. I realize I am in the area of Manzanar War Relocation Center, one of the prison camps where Japanese Americans were taken during World War II. By "in the area," I mean a four-hour drive, because Manzanar is in the middle of nowhere. I extend my trip to make my first journey to nowhere.

Eighty years ago, my grandparents traversed this same route. While I travel in an air-conditioned rental car and listen to '80s music on the way, they were forced onto a train, and then a bus, before arriving at the gates of Manzanar. I'm guessing their journey took eight to ten hours. At the time, my grandmother was twenty-nine and my grandfather was thirty-five. They had with them my three uncles, then ages six years, two years, and four months. They also had my grandfather's parents, one of whom was in a wheelchair. The military allowed them one suitcase per person.

I arrive at Manzanar on a Sunday afternoon, and I'm greeted by a friendly ranger from the National Park Service, which oversees the site. He shows me a registry with the name of every internee, and I discover that my grandparents were assigned to block 25, barracks 12, apartment 1. Each "apartment" was 20 × 25 feet, which meant that when my dad was born just over a year later, the eight family members shared 500 square feet. That works out to just over 60 square feet per person. The American Correctional Association currently calls for a minimum of 70 square feet per incarcerated person.

The friendly park ranger points in the direction of block 25, now a vacant piece of land several hundred yards away from the visitor center. I walk to the patch of land that used to hold the tiny room where my family slept. I'm surprised by the amount of glass and porcelain shards strewn around the ground. On reflection, it makes sense. When the government closed Manzanar, they hastily deconstructed the temporary facilities, and any remaining personal items were likely an afterthought. Because 16 U.S.C. § 470ee makes it a federal crime to remove items from public lands, I may or may not have taken a porcelain shard from the spot of land on which block 25, barracks 12, apartment 1 once stood. If I am ever prosecuted, I will plead for mercy under the circumstances.

When I return to the camp museum, the park ranger points me to a display of the *Manzanar Free Press*, the paper that reported the daily rhythms of life in the camps. The ranger moves over to his computer and pulls up some issues that mentioned my family. One of them connects to a story my grandma told me years ago. My uncle, who was two at the time, was playing on a truck when he fell off and was terribly injured. My grandma, seven months pregnant with my dad, had to carry my uncle to the hospital, where he remained for many days but ultimately managed a complete recovery. At the end of his hospitalization, my grandparents took out an ad in the *Manzanar Free Press*:

> IN APPRECIATION: To the hospital staff and workers, for
> their untiring care and kindness to our son, Akio, during his
> long confinement at the hospital, and to our many friends
> for their "omimai"—our heartfelt gratitude and appreciation.

My grandparents and the rest of the family had their own long confinement. In February 1944, after two years at Manzanar, they were transferred to a harsher facility at Tule Lake after my grandfather raised questions about their incarceration as American citizens. When the war ended, they relocated to the East, and my grandfather took a job with Westinghouse in Philadelphia. Grandpa Tai never recovered from the internment; he died in 1958 at the age of fifty-one.

My grandma Lily raised five kids in poverty as a single mom; she died in 2013 at the age of ninety-nine.

In 1988, President Reagan signed legislation that gave $20,000 to surviving Japanese Americans who had been interned. It wasn't much money—I think my grandmother bought some new kitchen cabinets. But the act also came with a formal apology from the president:

> The legislation that I am about to sign provides for a restitution payment to each of the 60,000 surviving Japanese-Americans of the 120,000 who were relocated or detained. Yet no payment can make up for those lost years. So, what is most important in this bill has less to do with property than with honor. For here we admit a wrong; here we reaffirm our commitment as a nation to equal justice under the law.

The apology meant a great deal to my grandmother. Her response was even more powerful. She forgave.

After a quick lunch meeting across campus, I return to my office to find Jennifer Chang's final independent study slid under my door. I pick it up and begin reading. I am stunned.

Jennifer's thesis, which had started as a sophomoric gloss of Augustine, has transformed into an incisive argument that raises subtle points I had never considered. She persuasively critiques some of the leading Augustine scholars. She still very much disagrees with Augustine's argument. But she has learned *how* to disagree. It is a fantastic paper. And she has included a note at the end thanking me for pushing her to think and write more clearly.

I am not quite sure how to process this moment. On the one hand, it feels like the kind of breakthrough that teachers experience far less frequently than we would like to believe. On the other hand, I quickly realize I have made the same kind of absolutist judgments about Jennifer I had critiqued in her writing—she was not teachable; she would undoubtedly produce a long-form diatribe; she was destined to be ineffectively brilliant. But that was not the case. In fact, thinking back more carefully on Jennifer's last few office visits with me, I begin to realize that more than her writing had changed. Her tone had softened; she had begun to ask more sophisticated and more nuanced questions; she was less combative and more engaging. Come to think of it, even her perfect posture had eased a bit.

I sometimes remind my students that we are all works in progress, all of us are fighting our own battles and blind spots, and all of us could use a little more grace and forgiveness. And today I am reminded that this includes not only Jennifer Chang but also me.

It also occurs to me that our capacity to forgive depends in part on our capacity to see ourselves as both in need of forgiveness and able to be forgiven. If you think you are perfect and have never wronged another person, it would be hard to persuade you that you should forgive the imperfect people who wrong you. On the other hand, if you see yourself as tainted to the point of being unforgivable, you may be unsure of why your forgiveness of someone else would even matter.

Fortunately, we don't need to look far to find exemplars of forgiveness in the world—people who have endured the unthinkable yet have chosen to forgive or look past the wrongs committed against them. The Amish may not command our respect as "sturdy yeomen" with their "idiosyncratic separateness." But in Nickel Mines, Pennsylvania, they inspired and confounded the nation with their powerful display of forgiveness toward the gunman who killed their children in a one-room schoolhouse. So, too, the family members of those massacred by a white supremacist during their Bible study at Mother Emanuel AME Church in Charleston, South Carolina. Or Charlie Singleton in response to the drunk Marine. Not everyone is able to forgive, and when it comes to the most egregious harms and abuses, forgiveness, if it comes at all, will be messy, imperfect, and piecemeal. It is natural to struggle with forgiveness in our own lives, especially in a world weighted by transgressions, vitriol, recklessness, and even evil. But we might still be comforted and inspired by acts of forgiveness that reveal the best of humanity in the worst of circumstances.

Can We Be
Friends?

Friendship is the hardest thing
in the world to explain.

Muhammad Ali

May is my favorite month of the year. Classes are over, and even though grading awaits, it's not the same pressure as December. May is also when I can play golf again in moderately pleasant conditions.

Golf is my life activity with the worst ratio of past effort to present performance. I started playing when I was ten. Some summer days, before I was old enough to drive, my mom would drop me off at the course in the morning and I would play 36 holes before calling her to come pick me up. Sometimes I would get annoyed when she couldn't come right away because she was finishing up work or making dinner or completing some other sacrificial act that allowed me to play golf all day long. Then after we returned home and started eating dinner, I'd give my parents the full play-by-play. *Tee shot on the first hole went a little left, but I hit a great five iron onto the fringe and got up and down for a par. Second hole, the wind was in my face, and it's that really long par 3, you know the one, Dad? Picked too much club and airmailed the green. . . .*

Can you imagine anything more boring than hearing the color commentary of someone else's mediocre golf game? Whenever my son Sam starts talking me through one of his ornate Lego creations and my attention starts to drift a bit, I remind myself that the apple doesn't fall far from the tree and I could be listening to him narrate an entire round of golf.

These days, I only play golf a handful of times each year. I usually manage a round or two with Gary. Golf is a good activity for Gary and me because we stick to small talk rather than pressing on each other's philosophical priors or arguing about faculty politics. I am reminded in these interactions that real friendship depends on a blend of shallow and deep. I'm not really friends with people who are shallow all the time. But the people who *only* go deep with me aren't my close friends either. We may share an intellectual connection or enjoy each other's company, but we're not really friends. Real friends can go deep and challenge each other but also sometimes hang out and do nothing except make small talk. Or play golf.

Gary and I usually play the public course near campus. It is in fairly good shape, and the greens are decent. And you can't beat the price. The downside is the course can get pretty crowded, but if we tee off early enough, we can usually get around without too much delay.

Today, we are joined by Jack Cunningham. Jack had reached out to me a few weeks ago about scheduling a round at his club, but I had countered with the idea of having him join Gary and me at the public course. It's a bit of a social experiment—pairing my law school colleague with my church friend and seeing if we can all get along.

I am counting on the small talk to keep us grounded. I have heard stories about people closing business deals or negotiating contracts on the golf course. I don't understand that at all. I am too busy chasing my ball around and cussing under my breath to talk seriously with anyone around me. Small talk, sure, but nothing that requires me to think. The point of golf is not to think.

The front nine goes reasonably well. Jack is riding in a cart, and Gary and I are walking. But Jack is a social guy, and he cruises alongside us as we walk up the fairways. We don't talk politics, which means that Jack avoids railing against "the liberals." Instead, he and Gary connect a bit over golf—they both learned to play in their late twenties, and both of them have struggled with swings that fight against the muscle memory of too many years of Little League baseball.

Everyone seems to be having fun today. After nine holes, Gary has a slight lead on me. Jack, by far the worst golfer in our group and beset with an incurable slice, is ten strokes back.

We stop at the turn for a quick bite and then start the back nine. Gary uncharacteristically yanks two in a row out of bounds off the tenth tee, each shot duck-hooking into the empty parking lot that lines the left side of the hole. He is clearly unhappy as he reloads for a third attempt to get the ball in play.

"Guess you are more to the left than you thought, eh, Gary?" Jack needles.

It's the kind of dumb golf joke that recreational golfers feel compelled to make, like "Worst three words in golf: 'you're still away.'" If you play a lot of golf, you learn to ignore these jokes.

Gary does not play a lot of golf.

"Hey, man, do you mind?" he snaps back at Jack. "You're not exactly setting any records today."

My social experiment is in jeopardy.

I think for a moment of how to intervene and decide to double down on the golf humor. "Don't worry, Gary. Jack's always so far to the right he has trouble seeing anyone else."

Not to brag, but it's a pretty good metaphor to come up

with on the spot. Gary chuckles, and Jack smirks. Disaster averted—and we continue on our way.

The sixteenth hole is a short par 3, about 140 yards. Gary and I hit wedges off the tee; Jack pulls out a fairway wood with an absurdly large club head. I'm sure it cost a fortune, and it looks ridiculous.

By this point in the round, Jack looks tired. He overswings and tops the ball, and we all watch it race down the short fairway, up to the fringe, across the green . . . and into the hole.

Suddenly, the three of us are celebrating like we've just won the Ryder Cup. Jack is beaming—it's his first hole in one in fifty years of golf. And Gary and I are the eyewitnesses to his special day.

We finish the round and stay for a couple of drinks. Each of us takes a moment to recount Jack's hole in one to the bartender—sometimes it is okay to give the play-by-play. More importantly, our day has been a reminder that the ordinary moments in life matter in sustaining existing friendships and embracing new ones. Nobody solved any of the world's problems, but Jack and Gary walked away with an experience they will never forget and a slightly better appreciation for one another.

Of course, these kinds of connections don't have to be over golf. You might hate golf or find it an obnoxiously privileged activity that's bad for the environment. Maybe your thing is cycling or going on walks or playing chess. Or perhaps you are into gaming or watching sports or playing music. Whatever it is, find something to create ordinary moments in life. And then use that something to pursue the ordinary interactions with others that precede and sustain genuine friendship.

Thursday is the last day of Law and Religion, and the last class I will teach this year. I have some parting shots for my students. I tell them I love teaching this class, not only because it's where I focus my research and writing, but also because it covers a lot of ground where the law runs out. Many of the topics we've covered this semester lie at the intersection of law, culture, and society and lack easy or obvious answers about what comes next.

I tell my students this is the fun part of lawyering, and it's also why lawyers get paid a lot of money. Plenty of people can memorize facts and formulas, but those won't get you very far when the law is unclear. It's one of the reasons I think a course like Law and Religion belongs in a law school curriculum. We are not just learning trivia; we are learning how to confront the murkiness. This is the stuff of legal practice. You argue the cases as best you can, distinguish unhelpful precedents, highlight the key facts, and tell the best possible story. And more often than you sometimes think or read on social media, there will be space for really good arguments and really good thinking.

The downside, of course, is that when the law is this unclear, you start to worry about arbitrary outcomes. At this point, some people give up. But I think the best lawyering comes from those who can push themselves to the edges of the law and raise hard questions when they encounter ambiguities and inconsistencies. That's hardest to do when you agree with the status quo. So I tell my students to find the cases and ideas they think are best and then force themselves to figure out the best arguments on the other side. And I also encourage them to be generous to those who come to different views about what the law is or should be.

This feels like an increasingly urgent task in our society. There are plenty of ideologues out there who are just trying to advance their own agendas, law be damned. But I think most lawyers are trying to take this stuff seriously, and I hope my students will choose to be these kinds of lawyers. In the midst of growing fracture and polarization, the world certainly needs these kinds of lawyers.

I close by telling them that while the law is important, it is not nearly the most important thing in their lives. But it will often try to claim that mantle. It will take as much of your time—and your soul—as you are willing to give it. Occasionally, I will encounter a student who has a little too much life in the work-life balance and could stand to work harder. But most of my students err in the other direction. They will be tempted to work so hard that they risk forgetting what they really care about.

A few weeks later, after the end-of-semester cramming, followed by exams, followed by grading, we get to graduation. It's one of the more emotionally complex ceremonies marking the passage of time. There's even a Supreme Court opinion reflecting on the significance of high school graduation: "Everyone knows that in our society and in our culture high school graduation is one of life's most significant occasions."

It's another Justice Kennedy-ism: *everyone knows*. Also, that case involved a *middle* school graduation. I doubt everyone knows middle school graduation is one of life's most significant occasions. Most kids are probably just hoping their parents don't embarrass them.

Law school graduation feels weightier. It's not quite as momentous as a wedding or a funeral. But for most of the people walking across the stage, it will be their last time donning a cap and gown, the last ceremony of many such ceremonies to mark the end of an era. Most of them are finishing 19th grade; for a few who finished PhDs before law school, it's closer to 26th grade. For everyone, it's a long time to have been in school.

Law school graduation also marks the stark transition from student to professional. Almost everyone is heading off to be a lawyer, and almost everyone will start studying for the bar exam in just a few days. All of this makes graduation more of a shared experience, the culmination of three very long years that started with the indoctrination of first-year cold calls and, at least for my students, a case about cannibalism.

At our school, the faculty sit on the stage, facing the students, who have their friends and family cheering them on from behind them. The ceremony starts with some canned speeches, most of which I could do without. But the next part is usually worth the wait. One by one, the students walk across the stage in front of us to receive their diploma from the dean. Three seconds of unvarnished pride and joy are reflected in each face that crosses the stage. I know some of these faces well; others I haven't seen since my orientation talk three years earlier. I'm not an overly emotional person, but I'll admit to feeling something in that moment the faculty rise to applaud the graduating class after the last diploma is awarded. Then we process out of the building. The faculty lead the way past the rows of parents, grandparents, and friends.

After we exit the auditorium, we walk toward the reception. The next few minutes will be some of the best and worst moments of the year. They are the worst because, as with most professors, my social skills max out at a six-person dinner party unless I have an assigned role. Give me a large crowd and call me "speaker" and everyone else in the room "audience," and I'll be fine. Or put me in front of a classroom where I am the teacher and everyone else is a student. But stick me in an open room with hundreds of people I don't know, and you have created my social nightmare.

On the positive side of the ledger, enduring the reception means I get to meet the friends and family of the students I have taught over the past three years. It's worth some awkwardness to meet Kim Riley's parents and share with them how extraordinary Kim has been as my research assistant. Or to have Rodney Livingstone introduce me to his fiancée and have her tell me that Rodney has spoken often of the seminar he took with me during his second year. Or to meet Lizzie Davenport's parents in person, after some difficult phone calls with them during a particularly challenging mental health stretch for Lizzie that ended with the right counselor and a necessary reset in her stress management. These students have worked hard and some of them have overcome great obstacles, and this is for them the culmination of a long process.

As I walk away from the reception, it occurs to me that graduation also restructures the relationship of teacher and student. After today, we become former teacher and former student. That also opens the possibility of a new form of friendship. I realize that friendship doesn't emerge with all of my former students, not even all of the ones I've gotten to know well. But every so often, someone takes a job locally and checks in periodically, and after a few years, we've shifted from teacher and student to something closer to friends. Maybe one day Jennifer Chang and I will even be friends.

After the reception, I bump into Brenda on the way back to my office. She looks uncharacteristically melancholy, and when I ask her what's wrong, she invites me into her office. We spend a few minutes reliving graduation and sharing a laugh over the dean's canned remarks. I tell her about meeting Lizzie's parents, and she recounts a few of her own conversations with parents. We both agree the reception was awkwardly worthwhile.

Then she lowers her voice and says, "I'm leaving the law school."

I have been caught off guard by a few conversations and announcements over the past year—Kim Riley sharing the news of the protest against the Stanford professor, Joseph Villario breaking down in my office, a rare compliment from my son Sam. But nothing is quite as startling as hearing this news from Brenda. I had always thought this job was made for people like Brenda.

Brenda tells me she is yearning to be more engaged with work in the community. Yes, her books have felt important, and people have told her they "make a difference." But she

thinks she can be more effective advocating for the people in
the community who lack access to power and resources. The
law school comes with too much administrative bureaucracy,
too many student protests, and, of course, too many faculty
meetings. I remind Brenda that The Seat will now be forever
mine, but I know it won't mean as much.

After a few more minutes talking to Brenda, I start walking
toward my office. Down the hallway, I spot some boxes outside
of Gary's office, and I feel a tinge of dread. Is Gary also
leaving? Perhaps he's been recruited away by another school?
Maybe UCLA is finally getting back at us for winning Gary on
the entry-level market. Next year's faculty meetings are already
going to be bad enough without Brenda. Am I also losing my
post-meeting walks with Gary? Am I running out of friends?

I peek into Gary's office and see him pulling books off the
shelf. It's clear he knows I have no idea what's going on, and
he seems to revel in my uncertainty, willing to wait me out
until I ask him about the boxes. I somehow manage to ask the
question without words, just a facial expression that he has
come to know. He responds, with a bit of a smirk, "Associate
dean." It turns out the dean asked him last week, and Gary
agreed yesterday to the three-year stint. He's only moving up
one floor to the dean's suite.

I am a little hurt that neither Gary nor Brenda consulted
me about their momentous decisions. But mostly I am thinking
to myself, *Why would Gary want to be associate dean?* It's a ton
of work, and you have to put up with all of your colleagues
griping or asking you for special goodies they're too afraid to
ask for from the dean. Plus, Gary will probably have to give
speeches to alumni about "equality" and "justice."

At this point, Gary reminds me that he is perfectly fine with our vaguely defined values. Maybe they don't make sense, but they work well enough. Students come, teachers stay, and alumni give money. And, Gary says, this job is a privilege. Yes, he wishes his students protested less and read more. But he likes what he does, and he wants to make this place as good as it can be. I should want that too, he tells me.

At dinner later that evening, Caroline and I are talking about our upcoming summer vacation. Like most years, we will rent a house in Ocean Isle Beach, North Carolina, a few miles away from Wilmington. She is excited about the beach, and I am excited about the local coffee shop, Surf and Java. I remember one of the things I like about Surf and Java is never having to guard a table for extended pondering. I am just getting my coffee and leaving to walk toward the beach. I won't even have exams to grade because, unlike during Christmas break, I will have finished my grading before we leave for our vacation.

I am hoping that a few weeks away will give me greater clarity about whether I will develop a plan like Brenda's or whether I will stay put, trying to work toward deeper thinking and greater empathy with my students. Something tells me that Gary, with all of his unsatisfying ambiguity and pragmatism, is probably right about the unique opportunities that come with this job. We work through the murkiness of life and law with students and colleagues, engaged in a shared effort to learn from one another. Unlike the fast-paced world into which most of our students are headed, in this place, we can lower the stakes and lengthen the conversations. We can practice empathy and disagreement with people who are different from us—perhaps some of whom are even friends in the making.

Asking the Right Questions

Two weeks later, I find myself sitting on the beach at Ocean Isle. The coastal town is comfortably familiar—sparsely populated with seasonal renters like us interspersed among a few hundred residents. Aside from Surf and Java, Ocean Isle has a couple of reliable restaurants and a crowded tiki bar we never visit. We spend most of the time in our rental house, listening to the ocean waves and enjoying the breeze. I don't love the beach like Caroline does, but I enjoy the change of scenery, especially in the middle of the hot, humid summer back home. And I don't have any meetings or deadlines.

One of the best parts about this annual pilgrimage is going completely offline. No computers, phones, or tablets; no texts, emails, or social media. Not everyone has a job that lets them put away all tech for a week, but with enough planning I can pull it off.

A few things happen over the course of this week offline. First, shockingly, life goes on without me. The world does not need me as much as I think it does. Sometimes our beach vacation coincides with the end of the Supreme Court's term, and once or twice I have missed calls from journalists looking for a comment on a blockbuster opinion about law and religion. But being offline means I am oblivious to these developments, and instead of speed-reading a few hundred pages of opinions, I am walking with Hana or throwing a football with Sam. For me, that's a pretty good tradeoff.

A second result of being offline for a week is that when I return to my inbox, I discover my rate of unanswered email over time follows something of a decay curve. The fewer emails I answer, the fewer arrive. The volume diminishes quickly enough that stepping away from email for a week is not even close to seven times as daunting as stepping away from email for a day. After a few days, most people learn to wait or find answers to their questions some other way.

Every year, a few days into my time offline, I realize that in addition to all of the emails and Supreme Court decisions I have ignored, I have also missed all of the other news. Because Caroline and I make our kids join us in our fast from technology, nobody else knows any news either. We have no idea what's happening in the rest of the country and around the world. We don't even know what's happening in the rest of Ocean Isle Beach outside of the five or six houses we see on the street where we rent. Our world has gotten smaller.

Of course, there is a certain artificiality to this tech-free week at the beach. For one thing, it's not sustainable. I suppose I could avoid the news if I had a different job. But teaching law gives me some responsibility for knowing what's going on in the world. A second challenge is that the beach—or at least this beach—is fairly homogenous. Actually, quite homogenous. When I look at the people around me, I realize that I bring most of the racial diversity. The rentals here are also pricey enough that there is not much income diversity either. We are not at one of the fancy beaches where everyone is wealthy, but nobody here is poor. Mostly, it's a bunch of people like us who call ourselves "upper middle class" instead of acknowledging that anyone with the time and money to take a beach vacation at Ocean Isle has probably surpassed the income boundaries of even the "upper" part of "middle class."

There is another way that the beach collapses difference. Nobody here has any social roles. We're all just people at the beach. There are still observable differences, of course—young and old, quiet and obnoxious, beautiful and not so beautiful. And you can tell that not everyone here shares the same politics or religion. The house across the street is flying an American flag, and three of the four vehicles in the driveway are pickups. Three houses down in the other direction is a younger couple driving a Prius. I overheard them talking on one of my morning walks, and it is safe to assume they won't be buying a pickup anytime soon.

The artificiality of the beach—the smallness of my world here—also opens my mind to a different set of questions. I think a lot more about the people immediately proximate to me, which in this case happens to be Caroline and our kids. I have far fewer decisions to make, and most of them are inconsequential—walk back to the beach or play a board game; sit outside or take a nap.

Most days at the beach, the universe of people I encounter ranges between my family and my family plus Lilian the barista at Surf and Java. Some days I say hello to our neighbors, including the people with the American flag and the people with the Prius. Nobody ever asks hard questions about politics or law.

People are also for the most part staying to themselves and not seeking conflict. Yesterday, the college kids in the house down the street drank too much and set off some illegal fireworks. But nobody confronted them or called the police. Nobody cares. Everybody jaywalks. In this slightly artificial world, law doesn't matter as much because the possibility of serious conflict seems quite distant.

I also realize I am not mad at any of these people. After a couple of days of sitting outside on our balcony, I know more about the actual lives of the people in the house next door than I do about any of the partisan strangers I encounter on social media. And perhaps because I have been observing the ordinariness of these people's lives, I tend to assume the best about them. Or at least, I don't assume the worst about them.

On Saturday morning, we pack up the van and head back home to a world full of news, people, and problems. I am glad to have had this break. But real life for most people isn't the beach. It's instead full of nuance and complexity, of conflict and disagreement, of the local mixing with the global and everything in between. It's a world of hard questions without easy answers. But as my time at the beach has reminded me, it's also a world where a little bit of familiarity—and a little bit of empathy—can still go a long way.

Reflection Guide

AUGUST: HOW DO WE LEARN EMPATHY?

What are some of the limits of your own experiences that make it difficult for you to understand or empathize with different viewpoints or ideas?

How do you balance speaking truthfully and authentically with showing care and respect for others around you? Can you think of examples where you have fallen short by (1) speaking truthfully but uncharitably or (2) speaking charitably but untruthfully or inauthentically?

When do you find yourself most and least empathetic toward people you don't know? What accounts for those differences?

Do you find it easier to empathize across difference with someone you don't know or someone familiar to you? Does it depend on what kind of difference separates you?

Have you experienced yourself or others saying things they wouldn't say in public when the assumption is that everyone listening shares the same beliefs and values? Is it important to keep the tone and substance of our public and private speech consistent, or should there be times when we can cut loose and "say what we really believe"?

How would you define *bias*? What do you find helpful or unhelpful about discussions around bias? How do you know when you or others around you hold such bias?

SEPTEMBER: CAN WE KNOW WHAT'S FAIR?

How do our own experiences help us decide what is fair?

In what ways do you find yourself treated differently than others? Do you think this is a product of unfairness, or something else?

Have you ever been let off the hook after breaking the law? Was that fair? Why or why not?

How does our ability or lack of ability to empathize determine
what we think is fair?

Do you agree with Brenda that without specificity about
what we believe (good and bad), the only plausible option is
a purely procedural approach that sets the rules of the game
and requires everybody to comply with them? In a pluralistic
society, is it possible to specify what is good versus what is bad?

Think about the institutions in your life—your family, work,
church, school. Is there clarity about what they value? How
do those values shape what is decided as fair within that
institution?

OCTOBER: WHAT HAPPENS WHEN WE CAN'T COMPROMISE?

What do we do with the fact that compromise isn't always possible? That the law picks winners and losers derived from sometimes arbitrary lines? How does this change the way we act or think?

How do you balance competing priorities when it's impossible to satisfy all of them?

As a society, have we made misguided decisions about competing values?

Learning to Disagree

How do you navigate situations in which there must be one clear winner and one clear loser?

How do you find empathy for those with whom you feel compromise is impossible?

How comfortable are you with the idea that the law makes certain choices for us? Do our current laws restrain too much or too little?

Think of a time when you were not able to compromise. What was difficult about that experience? In what ways was the inability to compromise a good thing?

NOVEMBER: CAN WE HAVE DIFFICULT CONVERSATIONS?

Where do you draw the line between difficult conversations and those you are not willing to have?

Can you think of a time when you pushed yourself to engage with another person whose views significantly differed from yours on a matter of importance? What was the outcome? Did your views change at all?

To what extent do you think you should engage with those who hold different worldviews than you do? Do you think you do this too often or too rarely in your everyday life?

Do you think it is ever effective to shut down debate completely? If so, how do you determine when that time has come?

How do you balance personal connections and intellectual connections with your loved ones? Do you find it difficult to separate the two?

Who do you need to start talking with again? How would you begin the conversation?

Describe a time when you had a difficult conversation at the wrong time or with the wrong person. How can you know when it is the right time to have a difficult conversation?

Do you struggle most with patience, humility, or tolerance when navigating deep differences? What are some practical steps you could take to grow in this area?

DECEMBER: CAN WE SEE PEOPLE INSTEAD OF PROBLEMS?

What methods have you found effective for humanizing those who might otherwise be viewed as a problem in your life?

Can you think of an instance when you failed to treat someone as a person rather than as a problem?

Describe a time when you were surprised by a person's story, competence, or character. Why was it surprising?

In which areas in your life do you need to remember the humanity of people?

What makes it hard for you to remember the humanity of people?

JANUARY: CAN WE TRUST FAITH?

In what do you place your faith?

What do you think is the appropriate connection between religion and patriotism? How has patriotism been used for good? How has it been harmful?

Are there certain components of national identity you think are essential for finding unity?

Think back to Jack Cunningham's comments about critical race theory and Tanya Mitchell's and Jeff Carpenter's comments about Christians. How do these two perspectives reflect current divides in America?

What role should the law play in judging the sincerity or validity of a particular religion?

When has your lack of understanding caused you to unfairly judge another for their words, actions, or beliefs? Have you been unfairly judged for yours?

Describe a time when you have doubted your faith. How did you navigate that doubt?

FEBRUARY: CAN ANYTHING BE NEUTRAL?

Do you think the two cases mentioned in the chapter—the snake handler and the Amish community—were rightly decided? What principle or rationale are you using to guide your opinion?

Is neutrality possible in law or education?

What is the difference between a lack of neutrality and a lack of nuance?

What is a current issue where you tend to lack nuance in your viewpoint?

MARCH: WHERE IS THE LINE BETWEEN WRONG AND EVIL?

How do you differentiate between wrong and evil? What have you considered "evil" that may instead just be "wrong"?

How does recharacterizing something as wrong as opposed to evil change how you think about the issue or the people who hold that "wrong" view?

Have you ever been in a situation like Joe where your views were shouted down by the loud majority? Have you been the loud majority? If you were the loud majority, do you think there may have been a better way to converse with the other side?

APRIL: IS FORGIVENESS POSSIBLE?

Do you think forgiveness is possible? Why or why not?

What are some examples of forgiveness you find challenging, inspiring, or problematic?

How do you balance forgiveness with change and accountability?

What are the impediments to forgiveness in your own life?

MAY: CAN WE BE FRIENDS?

What do you value in a friendship?

Learning to Disagree

Do you find more rewarding your relationships with those who are similar to you or with those who are different from you?

What do you think the importance is of befriending those who hold views that contradict your own?

Do you prefer friendships with a mix of deep and shallow interactions, or with more of one or the other?

Can you think of an example in which your empathy was tested in a friendship? What did you take away from that experience?

When it comes to your loved ones, how do you balance personal relationships with political disagreements? Do you find it difficult to separate the two?

How have your friendships shaped what you consider to be most important in your life?

What are the challenges and opportunities of cross-generational friendships?

FINAL QUESTIONS

What were some of the themes from the book that stood out to you?

When did you disagree with the author?

Did a specific story from the book leave an impression on you?
How did it affect you?

What are a few things you will take from this book moving
forward? What practical steps can you take after reading this
book?

Who in your life would benefit from reading this book?

Acknowledgments

I am privileged to work with amazing colleagues and students at Washington University in St. Louis. The law school environment that unfolds on the pages of this book bears some resemblances to Washington University's School of Law, but I have kept the details intentionally nondescript on the belief that the challenges and opportunities modeled in legal education cut across most peer institutions and have a broader applicability to many different social contexts.

I am grateful to a number of friends, colleagues, and students who read and commented on drafts of this manuscript, including Amin Aminfar, Christian Baker, Clare Carter, Marcus Cave, Nathan Chapman, Marc DeGirolami, Jon Endean, Ben Ewer, Francesca Frkonja, Mary Ellen Giess, Alice Gorman, Maisie Greene, Nathan Hall, Elizabeth Held, Dylan Hitchcock-Lopez, Ridge Hughbanks, Bethany Jenkins, Carolyn Kroenke, Won Lee, Laurie Maffly-Kipp, Kate Moran, Rachel Mattingly Phillips, Greg Mitchell, Seth Reid, Brent Roam, Shelby Saxon, Katy Schmidt, Alex Siemers, Richard Sims, Johanna Smith, AnneMarie Underwood, Olivia Wall, and Elijah Wiesman. Thanks to Grayson Cornwell for letting me include your family's story. I am also deeply appreciative of Matt Bray, Dirk Buursma, Devin Duke, Katie Painter, Paul Pastor, Webb Younce, and the entire team at Zondervan for their care with this book.

Three people deserve special thanks: John Siniff, who walked with me on this book from start to finish; John Hendrix, who helped me reframe the book the way it needed to be (and then provided illustrations!); and my agent, Susan Andreone, who believed in this book and helped me see it through to completion. Thanks also to Susan Andreone and Elizabeth Held for encouraging me to start my Substack, *Some Assembly Required*, where I drafted early versions of some of the material in this book.

For cheer and consolation along the way, I am indebted to my writing support group (Nii Addy, Andy Crouch, Andrea Dilley, Tish Harrison Warren, and Michael Wear) and the Whiskey Wednesday crew (John Hendrix, Andy Murphy, Karl Pollack, Paul Savage, and Abram Van Engen).

Lauren, Hana, and Sam, thank you for letting me share a few incomplete glimpses into your extraordinary lives and for putting up with all of my writing.

Caroline, I am sorry it took me so long to get you a book dedication, but I'm glad it's this one. You have walked with me through some of the highs and lows of my own disagreements—often with others and occasionally with you—and you have shown me how to navigate them with humor, love, and grace.

Notes

August: How Do We Learn Empathy?

4 **"Is today Tuesday? It depends":** For examples of the ambiguity of "Tuesday" in some legal contexts, see DeMarco Durzo Dev. Co. v. United States, 73 Fed. Cl. 731 (Fed. Cl. 2006): "For example, when someone speaks of 'a week from Tuesday' they are generally understood as referring to the following Tuesday. If one counted seven days from Tuesday by counting Tuesday as day one, they would find that 'a week from Tuesday' works out to the following Monday. That is certainly not the common understanding"; Steinmetz v. Signer, 23 Ind. 386 (Ind. 1864): "If the day of the month is disregarded, then the notice becomes entirely uncertain, for there were several Tuesdays in that month, and nothing to designate which one was meant. But 'May 18th' would be certain, and we should not hesitate to reject the day of the week as surplusage, and hold the notice sufficient to require the defendant to appear on the 18th."

7 **"*Dudley and Stephens* is nearly a rite of passage":** You can learn more about *Dudley and Stephens* in Allan C. Hutchinson, *Is Eating People Wrong? Great Legal Cases and How They Shaped the World* (New York: Cambridge University Press, 2011). I am indebted to Joshua Dressler for my thinking about this case and for much of my thinking about teaching criminal law. See Joshua Dressler, *Understanding Criminal Law*, 9th ed. (Durham, NC: Carolina Academic Press, 2022).

9 **"I like the case because it takes us to the limits of empathy":** The challenge of finding empathy across difference and uncertainty is no small thing, and it's easy to be uncharitable toward people and ideas you don't like. I explore more of these ideas in *Confident Pluralism: Surviving and Thriving through Deep Difference* (Chicago: University of Chicago Press, 2016).

16 **"I am not convinced that bias training is the right way":** The efficacy of implicit bias training has been much debated in recent years. For an overview of this debate, see Christine Ro, "The Complicated Battle over Unconscious-Bias Training," BBC, March 28, 2021; Tiffany L. Green and Nao Hagiwara, "The Problem with Implicit Bias Training," *Scientific American*, August 28, 2020.

September: Can We Know What's Fair?

23 **"Russian roulette known as Russian poker":** For an example of a second-degree murder conviction for death resulting from Russian poker, see *Commonwealth v. Malone*, 354 Pa. 180 (Pa. 1946).

25 **"Jennifer Axelberg was arrested for driving drunk":** The Minnesota Supreme Court rejected Jennifer Axelberg's necessity defense in *Axelberg v. Commissioner of Public Safety*, 848 N.W.2d 206 (Minn. 2014).

26 **"I learn about the drunk Marine from Charlie Singleton":** Although I rely mostly on composite characters in this book, the character of Charlie Singleton is based on a student from my 2019 Criminal Law class, Grayson Cornwell. See Neil Schoenherr, "Crime and Punishment: Two Students Embody Lessons Taught in Law School Class," Washington University: The Source, July 12, 2019.

28 **"I've heard enough stories from friends":** The issues surrounding municipal traffic and misdemeanor courts are explored in the Department of Justice's report on the Ferguson Police Department. See "Investigation of the Ferguson Police Department," United States Department of Justice Civil Rights Division, March 4, 2015. See also Thomas Harvey and Brendan Roediger, "St. Louis County Municipal Courts, For-Profit Policing, and the Road to Reforms," in *Ferguson's Fault Lines: The Race Quake That Rocked a Nation,* ed. Kimberly Jade Norwood (Chicago: American Bar Association, 2016), 57–74.

34 **"This week's review had been prompted by an incident":** Washington University's "Statement of Principle Regarding Freedom of Expression" was adopted on September 6, 2016, and is available on the school's website. The 9/11 protest occurred in September 2021. See Andrea Salcedo, "A Student Was Filmed Putting American Flags in a Trash Bag on 9/11. He Says He Was Protesting Islamophobia," *Washington Post,* September 14, 2021; Matthew Friedman and Ted Moskal, "WU Sanctions Alkilani with Probation, $500 Fine and Essay for Flag Removal, per Confidential Letter Publicized by College Republicans President," *Student Life,* October 22, 2021.

37 **"I worry that functionality without clarity":** For a more extended reflection on vague institutional references to "equality" and "justice," see my article titled "The Purpose (and Limits) of the University," *Utah Law Review* 5 (2018): 943–78. See also Steven D. Smith, *The Disenchantment of Secular Discourse* (Cambridge, MA: Harvard University Press, 2010), 26–33.

October: What Happens When We Can't Compromise?

42 **"certain zero-sum decisions are unavoidable":** The zero-sum nature of self-defense is a bit more complicated in states that recognize imperfect self-defense claims. See Joshua Dressler, *Understanding Criminal Law*, 9th ed. (Durham, NC: Carolina Academic Press, 2022).

43 **"But figuring out what is reasonable is not self-evident":** Like notions of fairness, our assessments of reasonableness are often less than satisfying. I explore some of these questions in my article titled "Beyond Unreasonable," *Nebraska Law Review* 99 (2020): 375–418.

43 **"Zimmerman's acquittal means that Trayvon Martin's death":** George Zimmerman was acquitted of second-degree murder charges in the death of Trayvon Martin under Florida's "stand your ground" laws. See Arian Campo-Flores and Lynn Waddell, "Jury Acquits Zimmerman of All Charges," *Wall Street Journal*, July 14, 2013; David G. Savage and Michael Muskal, "Zimmerman Verdict: Legal Experts Say Prosecutors Overreached," *Los Angeles Times*, July 14, 2013.

43 **"The key case involves Judy Norman":** Judy Norman's case is reported in *State v. Norman* 324 N.C. 253 (N.C. 1989).

45 **"But what about people like me who are allergic to the pets?":** For more on allergies and airplanes, see Jacqueline Swartz, "Should Cats Be Allowed on Airplanes?" CNN, December 8, 2022. Swartz advises, "One thing economy passengers can do is call the airline ahead of time and ask to reserve a seat at least five rows away from the nearest cat" because "the airline might know where the cats are located, since passengers who want to take their pets with them in the cabin must book the animal in advance."

47 **"Law students do not always like the idea":** My understanding of the connection between law and violence has been shaped by Robert Cover, "Violence and the Word," *Yale Law Journal* 95, no. 8 (July 1986): 1601–29. Cover notes how law's authority is rooted in violence. Law also restrains violence. In its best forms, it can prevent death, alleviate suffering, and maintain order.

November: Can We Have Difficult Conversations?

52 **"This unit is the most difficult sequence":** For an overview of some of the tensions of teaching sexual assault, see Jeannie Suk Gersen, "The Trouble with Teaching Rape Law," *New Yorker*, December 15, 2014.

54 **"the exchange illustrates how challenging classroom teaching can be":** My views on the complexity and contingency of teaching are influenced by Ken Bain, *What the Best College Teachers Do* (Cambridge, MA: Harvard University Press, 2004).

57 **"I also learned a lot as I watched him die":** It is hard to overstate how awful it is to watch a loved one die of lung cancer. During my dad's illness and death, I benefited from reading Paul Kalanithi, *When Breath Becomes Air* (New York: Random House, 2016); Atul Gawande, *Being Mortal: Medicine and What Matters in the End* (New York: Metropolitan, 2014); and Timothy Keller, *Walking with God through Pain and Suffering* (New York: Penguin, 2015). I also recommend Lydia Dugdale, *The Lost Art of Dying: Reviving Forgotten Wisdom* (New York: HarperOne, 2020), published after my dad died.

60 **"But it's like what David Foster Wallace says":** David Foster Wallace's famous fish and water example is from his 2005 commencement address at Kenyon College titled "This Is Water."

61 **"Maybe a reasonable place to start":** For an overview of the effects of racially discriminatory policies across generations, see Colin Gordon, *Mapping Decline: St. Louis and the Fate of the American City* (Philadelphia: University of Pennsylvania Press, 2008), and Richard Rothstein, *The Color of Law: A Forgotten History of How Our Government Segregated America* (New York: Liveright, 2018). See also Jemar Tisby, *The Color of Compromise: The Truth about the American Church's Complicity in Racism* (Grand Rapids: Zondervan, 2020).

61 **"But it should mean an openness to critique":** My description of the tensions of growing up in mostly white churches draws from my chapter titled "The Translator" in *Uncommon Ground: Living Faithfully in a World of Difference*, ed. Timothy Keller and John Inazu (Nashville: Thomas Nelson, 2020). I raise questions related to critical race theory and white evangelism in "Breaking Out of the White Evangelical Echo Chamber," *Christianity Today*, February 10, 2020.

62 **"A few years ago, I wrote a piece":** My opinion piece titled "How to Unite in Spite of Trump" ran in *USA Today* on December 22, 2016. The quotes from readers are taken from emails and letters I received in response to that piece and similar essays I have written (on file with author, in my folder labeled "Crazy Stuff").

December: Can We See People Instead of Problems?

71 **"I want my students to think about these questions":** For an alternative account of what happens in the seemingly routine liturgies of the courtroom, see Cover, "Violence and the Word."

January: Can We Trust Faith?

82 **"For some of my students, it's more traditional religious faith":** Some of my reflections in this chapter about faith draw from my article titled "Law, Religion, and the Purpose of the University," *Washington University Law Review* 94 (2017). See also C. Kavin Rowe, *One True Life: The Stoics and Early Christians as Rival Traditions* (New Haven, CT: Yale University Press, 2016). Rowe notes that "the human condition is such that you have to choose how to live from among options that rule one another out." And we make that choice trusting in things unseen: "we wager our lives, one way or the other" (p. 1) because "we cannot know ahead of the lives we live that the truth to which we devote ourselves is the truth worth devoting ourselves to" (p. 258).

82 **"But we read it for the questions it raises":** My introductory case in Law and Religion is *United States v. Kuch*, 288 F. Supp. 439 (D.D.C. 1968).

85 **"I am doing the brisk walk to a faculty workshop":** For a more over-the-top caricature of the faculty workshop than I could ever write, see Pierre Schlag, "The Faculty Workshop," *Buffalo Law Review* 60, no. 3 (2012): 807–22.

88 **"There have been modest efforts to expand the tent":** Tim Keller and I discuss the "Judeo-Christian" narrative in the United States in our introduction to *Uncommon Ground: Living Faithfully in a World of Difference*. Joseph Bottum's *An Anxious Age: The Post-Protestant Ethic and Spirit of America* (New York: Image, 2014) explores the cultural implications of the white Protestant middle class and its collapse.

89 **"I introduce the highlight of this class":** The patriotic video is titled "God Bless the USA by Lee Greenwood" (track 10 on *You've Got a Good Love Comin'* [Nashville: Universal Music Group, 1984]) and can be found on YouTube. There is even a "God Bless the USA" Bible, which touts "the Bible and the founding documents of America . . . together in one very unique Bible." See also Ed Kilgore, "The Problem with the Lee Greenwood Bible," *New York Magazine*, May 31, 2021; Esau McCaulley, "Frederick Douglass Knew What False Patriotism Was," *New York Times*, July 3, 2023. "Our country," writes McCaulley, "wants a certain version of the American story told and will laud anyone willing to tell it. But uncritical celebration is a limited and false definition of patriotism. Instead, recounting the full story of America and asking it to be better than it is can be an expression of love."

91 **"the Supreme Court ruled that the children":** The decision vindicating the right of the Jehovah's Witnesses to refuse to pledge allegiance to the flag is *West Virginia State Board of Education v. Barnette*, 319 U.S. 624 (1943), which overruled *Minersville School District v. Gobitis*, 310 U.S. 586 (1940). The best account of the legal efforts of the Witnesses during the 1930s and 1940s is Shawn Francis Peters, *Judging Jehovah's Witnesses: Religious Persecution and the Dawn of the Rights Revolution* (Lawrence: University of Kansas Press, 2000). The *Barnette* decision (and the Witnesses' alternate pledge) is discussed in Vincent Blasi and Seana V. Shiffrin, "The Story of *West Virginia Board of Education v. Barnette*," in *First Amendment Stories*, ed. Richard W. Garnett and Andrew Koppelman (New York: Foundation Press, 2011), 433–75.

95 **"some general references to mental health concerns":** Mental health concerns are a growing part of law school and higher education contexts more generally. Some of these concerns come from academic performance, but many others are exacerbated by personal relationships, family circumstances, loneliness, substance abuse, racism, sexism, activism, sanctimony, and self-doubt. See Jessica R. Blaemire, "Well-Being in Law School—Law Students Aren't OK," Bloomberg Law, February 3, 2023.

February: Can Anything Be Neutral?

100 **"*Swann v. Pack* is the Law and Religion version":** The snake-handling case is *State ex rel. Swann v. Pack*, 527 S.W.2d 99 (Tenn. 1975). The most authoritative account of snake-handling deaths in the United States found ninety-one deaths from 1919 to 2008. See Ralph Hood and W. Paul Williamson, *Them That Believe: The Power and Meaning of the Christian Serpent-Handling Tradition* (Berkeley: University of California Press, 2008). Most of those cases could not be independently verified due to a lack of documentation.

104 **"Our principal case today is *Wisconsin v. Yoder*":** The case is *Wisconsin v. Yoder*, 406 U.S. 205 (1972).

106 **"When it comes to clashes that emerge at the intersection":** Alasdair MacIntyre discusses the challenges of emotivism and value judgments in *After Virtue: A Study* *in Moral Theory*, 3rd ed. (Notre Dame, IN: University of Notre Dame Press, 2007). I explore similar concepts in "Law, Religion, and the Purpose of the University." Other helpful books along these lines are C. Kavin Rowe, *One True Life: The Stoics and Early Christians as Rival Traditions* (New Haven, CT: Yale University Press, 2016), and Jonathan Haidt, *The Righteous Mind: Why Good People Are Divided by Politics and Religion* (New York: Vintage, 2013).

106 **"I assign a somewhat dated but smartly written article":** Russell Shorto's article is "How Christian Were the Founders?," *New York Times Magazine* (February 11, 2010). In 1996, conservative activist Ralph Reed famously quipped, "I would rather have a thousand school board members than one president and no school board members" (quoted in Michelle Goldberg, "Why the Right Loves Public School Culture Wars," *New York Times*, May 3, 2021).

March: Where Is the Line between Wrong and Evil?

116 **"Law and Religion class turns to three Supreme Court cases":** The three cases are *Reynolds v. United States*, 98 U.S. 145 (1878); *Davis v. Beason*, 133 U.S. 333 (1890)—challenging Idaho's oath test; and *Mormon Church v. United States*, 136 U.S. 1 (1890). For a powerful reflection on the Mormon persecution, see Frederick Mark Gedicks, "The Integrity of Survival: A Mormon Response to Stanley Hauerwas," *DePaul Law Review* 42, no. 1 (Fall 1992): 167–73.

120 **"Utah recently changed its law criminalizing bigamy":** The changes to Utah's bigamy law are reported in Harmeet Kaur, "Bigamy Is No Longer a Felony in Utah," CNN, May 12, 2020.

121 **"Justice Kennedy gives us a great deal of":** You can read Justice Kennedy's approach to free exercise and LGBTQ rights in *Masterpiece Cakeshop, Ltd. v. Colorado Civil Rights Commission*, 138 S. Ct. 1719 (2018). Subsequent decisions on related issues include *Fulton et al. v. City of Philadelphia, Pennsylvania*, 141 S. Ct. 1868 (2021), which upholds the free exercise claim of a Catholic adoption agency against a city policy excluding them from recognized placement agencies based on the agency's refusal to place children with same-sex couples, and *303 Creative LLC et al. v. Elenis et al.*, 600 U.S. 570 (2023), which upholds the free exercise claim of a website designer against a Colorado antidiscrimination law. The 2022 Respect for Marriage Act, Public Law No. 117–228 (12/13/2022) recognizes the legality of same-sex and interracial marriages and repeals the 1996 Defense of Marriage Act, which excluded same-sex marriage from marriages recognized as legally valid under federal law.

131 **"look for something good about the people you find most wrong":** My suggestion to look for the good in political leaders you dislike is taken from comments I made in Tish Harrison Warren's column titled "10 New Year's Resolutions That Are Good for the Soul," *New York Times*, January 2, 2022.

April: Is Forgiveness Possible?

134 **"I hear about the controversy involving the Stanford professor":** The classroom incident and protests involved Professor Michael McConnell at Stanford Law School. Professor McConnell read a historical quote from Patrick Henry that included the n-word, preceding it with a warning and following it with a condemnation. This incident came only a few days after the murder of George Floyd by a Minneapolis police officer, which triggered a summer of protests across the country. The details of McConnell's classroom incident are chronicled in Nick Anderson, "A Stanford Law Professor Read a Quote with the n-word to His Class, Stirring Outrage at the School," *Washington Post*, June 3, 2020. The protests against Professor McConnell spilled over to the *Washington University Law Review* because he had prepared a keynote article for a symposium on law and religion for which I served as the faculty editor, as explained in "Statement by the Undersigned Editors of Volume 97," *Washington University Law Review* 97, no. 6 (2020): i–iii, and my response, "Scholarship, Teaching, and Protest," *Washington University Law Review* 97, no. 6 (2020): vii–xiii.

141 **"reconciliation . . . requires both forgiveness and repentance":** My reflections on forgiveness and the pandemic can be found in my Substack post titled "Is It Time for Pandemic Forgiveness?," *Some Assembly Required*, November 4, 2022.

143 **"I arrive at Manzanar on a Sunday afternoon":** My account of my visit to Manzanar draws from my post titled "Glimpses of Family 10020: A Personal Pilgrimage to the Manzanar Internment Camp," *Some Assembly Required*, October 14, 2022. The Supreme Court upheld the constitutionality of the internment of Japanese Americans in *Korematsu v. United States*, 323 U.S. 214 (1944). The comments by Ronald Reagan were made on August 10, 1988, as he signed a bill providing restitution for the wartime internment of Japanese-American civilians. Several years ago, my cousin's husband, Gavin Cooper, self-published a beautifully designed reflection on the experience of my grandparents in the camps. That book concludes with a quote from my grandmother: "I don't hold any resentment against the government for being sent to the camps. I think they or someone panicked. We all know now that it wasn't necessary to put us there, but I don't resent them for what they did. I am still proud to be here and to be a citizen."

147 **"they inspired and confounded the nation":** For background on the story of Amish families forgiving the murderer of their children, see Joseph Shapiro, "Amish Forgive School Shooter, Struggle with Grief," NPR: *All Things Considered*, October 2, 2007. For the story of forgiveness after the Charleston massacre, see Mark Berman, "'I Forgive You.' Relatives of Charleston Church Shooting Victims Address Dylann Roof," *Washington Post*, June 19, 2015.

May: Can We Be Friends?

155 **"There's even a Supreme Court opinion":** The Supreme Court's reflection on graduation ceremonies is found in *Lee v. Weisman*, 505 U.S. 577, 595 (1992).

Epilogue: Asking the Right Questions

163 **"One of the best parts about this annual pilgrimage":** I am indebted to my friend Andy Crouch for the challenge that led to my annual week offline. See Andy Crouch, *The Tech-Wise Family: Everyday Steps for Putting Technology in Its Proper Place* (Grand Rapids: Baker, 2017). I've also benefited from Oliver Burkeman, *Four Thousand Weeks: Time Management for Mortals* (New York: Farrar, Straus and Giroux, 2021).

Epigraphs

August: Helen Demetriou, *Empathy, Emotion, and Education* (New York: Palgrave Macmillan, 2018), 2 (quoting Alfred Adler).

September: Daniel Handler, *The Carnivorous Carnival* (New York: HarperCollins, 2002), 188.

October: George Carlin, *Back in Town* (Home Box Office, 1996).

November: Jim Knight, Jennifer Ryschon Knight, and Clinton Carlson, *The Reflection Guide to Better Conversations: Coaching Ourselves and Each Other to Be More Credible, Caring, and Connected* (Thousand Oaks, CA: Corwin, 2015), 42 (quoting Wendell Berry).

December: C. S. Lewis, *The Weight of Glory* (New York: HarperCollins, 2009), 47.

January: Hebrews 11:1 (New International Version)

February: Howard Zinn, *You Can't Be Neutral on a Moving Train* (Boston: Beacon, 2018).

March: Bryan Stevenson, *Just Mercy: A Story of Justice and Redemption* (New York: Random House, 2014), 290.

April: Mother Teresa of Calcutta, *A Gift for God: Prayers and Meditations*, rev. ed. (San Francisco: HarperOne, 2003), 24.

May: Andrew O'Hagan, "Reflections on True Friendship," *New York Times Style Magazine*, November 23, 2016 (quoting Muhammad Ali).

From the Publisher

GREAT BOOKS

ARE EVEN BETTER WHEN THEY'RE SHARED!

Help other readers find this one

- Post a review at your favorite online bookseller

- Post a picture on a social media account and share why you enjoyed it

- Send a note to a friend who would also love it—or better yet, give them a copy

Thanks for reading!